Mexican Cooking

SUSAN LAMMERS
Editor

VICKI BARRIOS SCHLEY
ANGELO VILLA
Writers

LINDA HINRICHS
CAROL KRAMER
Designers

MICHAEL LAMOTTE
Photographer

AMY NATHAN
Food Stylist

SARA SLAVIN
Prop Stylist

EDITH ALLGOOD
Illustrator

CALIFORNIA
CULINARY
ACADEMY

Ortho Books

Publisher
Robert L. Iacopi

Editorial Director
Min S. Yee

Managing Editors
Jim Beley
Anne Coolman
Susan Lammers
Michael D. Smith
Sally W. Smith

Production Director
Ernie S. Tasaki

Editors
Richard H. Bond
Alice E. Mace

System Manager
Christopher Banks

System Consultant
Mark Zielinski

Asst. System Managers
Linda Bouchard
William F. Yusavage

Photographic Director
Alan Copeland

Photographers
Laurie A. Black
Richard A. Christman

Asst. Production Manager
Darcie S. Furlan

Associate Editor
Jill Fox

Production Editors
Don Mosley
Anne Pederson

Chief Copy Editor
Rebecca Pepper

Photo Editors
Kate O'Keeffe
Pam Peirce

National Sales Manager
Charles H. Aydelotte

Sales Associate
Susan B. Boyle

Operations Assistant
Gail L. Davis

Administrative Assistant
Georgiann Wright

Address all inquiries to
Ortho Books
Chevron Chemical Company
Consumer Products Division
575 Market Street
San Francisco, CA 94105

Copyright © 1985
Chevron Chemical Company
All rights reserved under
international and Pan-American
copyright conventions.

First Printing in July, 1985

1 2 3 4 5 6 7 8 9
85 86 87 88 89 90

ISBN 0-89721-053-0

Library of Congress Catalog Card
Number 85-070886

Chevron Chemical Company
575 Market Street, San Francisco, CA 94105

Danielle Walker *(left)* is chairman of the board and founder of the California Culinary Academy. **Vicki Barrios Schley's** knowledge of Mexican cooking is rooted in Mexico itself. From her relatives there, she learned about the foods and the cooking methods of Mexico's central interior and southwestern coastal region. Since then she has taught many classes across the country in Mexican cooking and has worked as a food consultant. **Angelo Villa,** a professor of Spanish at Valley College in Los Angeles, is a specialist in the history and development of Mexican cuisine.

The California Culinary Academy Among the forefront of American institutions leading the culinary renaissance in this country, the California Culinary Academy in San Francisco has gained a reputation as one of the most outstanding professional chef training schools in the world. With a teaching staff recruited from the best restaurants of Western Europe, the California Culinary Academy educates students from around the world in the preparation of classical cuisine. The recipes in this book were created in consultation with the Academy's chefs.

Acknowledgments

Copyeditor
Barbara Ferenstein

Photographers
Laurie Black, Academy photography
Fischella, photograph of
  Danielle Walker

Food Styling for Back Cover
Amy Nathan

Food Styling at the Academy
Jeff Van Hanswyk

Color Separations
Color Tech Corp.

Calligraphy
Chuck Wertman

Editorial Assistants
Anne Ardillo
Bil Lawrence

Consultants
Sara Godwin
Rita Held
Judith Whipple
Katherine Stimson

Special Thanks To

Elana Almanza
Lila Delgadillo Bane
Ron, Gabrielle, Veronica, Aaron, and Bret Barrios
Rugh Almanza Barrios
Diana Bohn
Memo Cobbledick
Walter Euyang
Ida Jaqua
Maria Morales
Mexican Museum of San Francisco
Carmen Salazar Parr
Kay and Brooks Pringle
Maria Guadalupe Progatsky
Joseph Puig
Josefina and Jo Rhodes
Peter Rodriguez
Don, Maryamber, Rico, and Tori Villa

Front Cover

Mexico is famous for its seafood. This kebab, composed of prawns, scallops, halibut, chiles, and vegetables, is coated with a buttery garlic sauce and then grilled over hot coals. See page 95.

Back Cover Photos

Upper left: Leeks, carrots, potatoes, onions, garlic, and herbs are just some of the ingredients that go into a rich veal stock.

Upper right: Two trouts garnished with lemon and parsley are ready to enter the fish poacher, where they will be simmered in white wine and herbs.

Lower left: Four Cornish game hens are arranged on a platter with baby carrots and green beans.

Lower right: Rosettes of whipped cream are piped onto a cake with a pastry bag and an open-star tip.

C O N T E N T S

Mexican Cooking

Mexican food and Mexican culture are intimately connected. The metate y mano, a flat stone grinder and muller for corn, is an important symbol of both.

Mexican Culture & Cooking

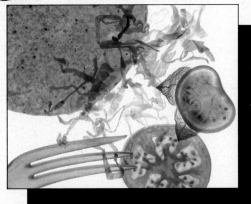

The cuisine of Mexico is as festive, rich, and hearty as its culture. Half of the food you eat probably had its origin in pre-Columbian America. Indeed, long before the Spanish expeditions to the New World, Mexico had developed a highly organized system of agriculture and a companion system of sophisticated culinary art. This book introduces you to both traditional and contemporary Mexican recipes. Along with the recipes, we share the secrets, the techniques, the traditions, and the marvels of authentic Mexican cooking.

THE CULINARY TRADITION

Mexico is a country with a long history of good cooking. It is a cuisine known for its unusual ingredient combinations, intriguing textures, and varied garnishes. Since the discovery of the New World, the culinary tradition of Mexico has influenced the way the entire world cooks. This book will expand that familiarity and deepen your appreciation for this great cuisine.

Pre-Hispanic Mexico was as rich in food resources as was the Old World: Many familiar foods—such as corn, chocolate, peanuts, pumpkins, tomatoes, pineapple, potatoes, dozens of different beans, chiles, papayas, avocados, sweet potatoes, sunflowers, chayotes, jicama, nopales, and vanilla—are native to Mexico, and there are dozens of others that haven't yet found favor beyond their own regions. The people of Mexico, always interested in enhancing their culinary art, were just as interested in the new foods the Spanish brought as the Europeans were in the wealth of new foods and plants sent back to Europe.

It is hard to imagine what cooking in Europe was like before the introduction of beans, squash, potatoes, tomatoes, and the other New World contributions.

Among the changes that the Spanish brought to Mexico, the most immediate and profound were caused by the livestock. (The only pre-Hispanic domesticated animals were the dog and the turkey.) The horse had an immediate effect; instilling fear in the Indian warriors, it was a pivotal factor in Cortés' first military campaigns. But of all the Spanish introductions, the pig was the catalyst for the greatest changes in the kitchen—not for the meat, popular as it must have been, but for the lard, which was used for frying.

Of all the indigenous plants, corn (or *maiz*) was the most important contributor to the sustenance of the people. Corn had been cultivated and tended for so long that, according to myth, it was the very stuff from which the gods created people.

More Than Recipes

This book gives you many Mexican recipes, both traditional and contemporary, some quick and easy, others more elaborate and challenging. In addition, we would like to tell you considerably more about Mexican cooking than just "how to do it."

In Mexico, there is still a direct and vital link between the production and consumption of food—a link that has become obscured for most of us. In this book, we hope to help rekindle some of the reverence for food and for the natural world that sustains us all. It is a reverence that has been and still is deeply rooted in the native culture.

Although mechanized farming methods are used in many areas of Mexico, much of the land remains unsuited to such methods, and yokes of oxen still plow rocky fields that would demolish most modern machines. The steep mountain slopes must also be farmed if the people are to eat. Such fields must be worked by men with the help of horses and burros, sturdy creatures that can take a firm foothold on a steep mountainside.

Buses and trucks may well be the most potent forces for change operating in Mexico today. The fish caught in Vera Cruz this morning will be in Mexico City (or even Guadalajara, 700 miles away) tomorrow. As the country's population and produce become more mobile, the cuisine changes. Already one finds dishes far from their original homes. Sometimes they've traveled well, remaining basically unchanged; but often it seems that they've brought only their names.

For all the forces that are tending to homogenize the cooking of Mexico, there are also strong forces working to maintain the centuries-old traditions. There are still large areas in the country that are out of reach of the road system, or can be reached only by primitive roads. The people in these areas of necessity live, eat, and cook largely with the same ingredients and the same methods that have been used since the time of the Aztec lords.

MEXICAN MEAL PATTERNS

Mexican eating patterns differ greatly from ours in the United States.

The Mexican day hinges on the *comida mexicana*, the midday dinner, usually taken in the early afternoon. The timing of meals varies between city and rural dwellers, but in all cases, the *comida*, followed by a restful siesta, divides the day into two distinct parts.

The basic meal pattern, indulged in to whatever extent individual affluence allows, starts with *desayuno*, usually café and a *pan dulce*, upon arising (or ideally even before arising). Often around 10:00 a.m. a second, more substantial, breakfast might be taken. This meal might consist of eggs, beans, tortillas, salsa, a beverage, and fresh fruit. If you have this big, late breakfast, you are likely to take your comida later in the afternoon. Or you might have a full-course Mexican brunch, midday, as your comida. There remains one more light meal, the evening *merienda*. For some, this evening meal is a soup or stew. For others, it might be leftovers just as it has been traditionally in farm homes in every country, and in Mexico it's common to wrap a tortilla around leftovers, making a taco or burrito. Many might have only *café con leche* and a sweet at the evening merienda, depending on their earlier daily fare.

On special occasions, or when entertaining, the merienda would be replaced by a *cena*, a light supper of two or three courses that might be served anytime between 8 p.m. and midnight.

There is an alternative to the meals described above. It is based still on the leisurely midday comida; however, the remainder of the day's eating might consist of only *antojitos*, "little whims," light snacks. Antojitos are a traditional manner of eating in Mexico as evidenced by the numerous vendors at every street corner (and often between as well). The variety of antojitos available is staggering. For the most part they are healthful, such as fresh fruits.

LA COMIDA MEXICANA

Our typical American dinner menu consists of soup or salad, a main dish, one or two vegetables, dessert, and a beverage. The traditional comida mexicana, however, consists of eight courses, each served separately and eaten leisurely at midday. The comida mexicana would include the following courses:

> *Aperitivo* (appetizer course)
> *Sopa* (soup course)
> *Sopa seca* (rice course)
> *Entrada* (the first entrée, a fish or cooked vegetable course)
> *Platillo fuerte* (the main course, which translates as "heavy plate"). This main-dish course would also include the *ensalada* (salad) and would be accompanied by tortillas or *bolillos* (dinner rolls)
> *Frijoles* (bean course)
> *Postre* (dessert course)
> *Café* (after-dinner coffee course)

This midday comida could also be a full-course brunch, a leisurely meal emphasizing the importance of egg dishes in the cuisine. The main dish of eggs would be garnished with salsa and sliced avocado, served with beans or rice and tortillas, and accompanied by fruits or melon, bak-

ery sweets, fresh juice, and Mexican coffee or Mexican hot chocolate.

If this were a weekend brunch or for guests it would probably include Mexican beer, margaritas, or sangría as well.

Such a meal in a fine restaurant can be a bit much, and the same is true when you are being entertained in an affluent private home. But in the everyday comida the portions served at each course are small. These meals may appear to be heavy meals, but they are taken midday and are usually lingered over. Also they are often followed by a siesta. Remember, the remaining meals of the day consist of "mini-meals" or antojitos (snacks), certainly a light and healthy way to round out the day's eating.

The rustic beauty and simplicity of the Mexican way of life make it a pleasant country to visit and get to know. Mexican food can provide a good introduction to the culture and traditions of Mexico.

Fresh fruits of all types are favored by Mexicans, especially on the beach, where they are sold by vendors at stands. Here you see a juicy mango that has been peeled, serrated, and impaled on a stick. Watermelon, pineapple, honeydew melon, and coconut are also favorites.

How Mexico Snacks

Eating in Mexico is a celebration! For Mexicans, food and fiesta minister to deep human needs that we often seem too ready to surrender to the instant, low-calorie lunch.

All of mankind's food must have started as finger food, and new finger snacks seem to appear in our markets almost daily; after all, knives and forks at the table are a rather recent innovation. The Mexican system of finger food must be a high point in variety and sophistication. We can assume that Montezuma and Cortés both ate with their fingers, but the tortilla gave Montezuma a neat advantage.

The ancient Mexicans also impaled their food on sticks (as we all still do) and used hollow quills as drinking straws. They would still feel at home with the food of today's Mexico.

Antojito is a wonderful word, meaning, literally, a "little whim." An older dictionary defines it as a "hankering" and that older American word certainly seems to fit. In Mexico, antojitos are generally served as single-dish snacks purchased from outdoor vending carts. Although *antojito* has often been incorrectly translated in the United States as an appetizer, it really is not an appetizer or first course. Perhaps, if it must be translated, it might best be thought of as an hors d'oeuvre.

On market day in the villages, in the open-air markets of the cities—wherever people gather—the food sellers are on hand. The more mobile vendors tour the neighborhood on regular routes, pausing where the crowds gather. Throughout Mexico, there are open-air restaurants and bars, as well as vendors, and the range of edibles runs from a full comida at top tourist prices to a cup of sweetened rice for a peso.

At the beach, if you can't find an empty *palapa* (a palm thatched shade) you can lie on your beach towels or rent chairs and woven mats from a small boy who immediately materializes at your elbow. Once you settle down with your choice of either sun or shade, the parade begins. The uninitiated will quickly realize the full impact of the word *antojito*: Vendors offer beer and soft drinks; delicious fish tidbits on a stick, or perhaps seviche (marinated fish); juicy mangoes on a stick, peeled and artfully serrated; watermelon in a square of paper; bakery goods; and all manner of *licuados* (fresh fruit drinks). *Elotes* are a special delicacy—young ears of sweet corn, neatly placed on a stick, dipped in heavy, sweet cream and sprinkled liberally with a sharp, crumbly cheese. There are snacks for all hours of the day and all moods of celebration: fruit and ices and melon and pineapple and green coconuts with the top hacked off for straws to reach the sweet-flavored milk.

In the folk tradition of Mexican cooking, food is classified as either hot or cold in a manner quite similar to the tradition in Chinese cooking. This classification has little or nothing to do with the temperature of the food, but rather with the effect of the food on the body. Hot foods are those that digest easily and produce heat in the body, while cold foods are difficult to digest and help lower body heat. According to Francis Toor in *The Mexican Folkways*, some foods considered hot are coffee, beef, honey and *pinole*, white pork, and rice. Boiled eggs, papaya, limes, and squash are cold. Fish is a cool food, even when it is served hot from the charcoal grill. Many foods—chicken, oranges, tomatoes, beans, and tortillas—are simply medium. Proper balance of hot and cold foods is considered necessary to good health.

THE MEXICAN KITCHEN

The Mexican colonial kitchen combined most of the best ingredients of the Old and New worlds, and the tools and techniques as well. There was a standup stove, if not always a chimney to go with it, and a beehive oven for baking bread. Animal power was used to grind the wheat that became common in the north and the sugar cane that was made into heavy syrup or solid *piloncillos*. Of course the kneel-down *metate* (grinding stone) was used for grinding *masa* (corn dough).

Many Mexican kitchens are still equipped with most of the household tools of pre-Conquest Mexico: the *metate* and *mano* (grinding stone and muller), *molcajete* (three-legged stone mortar for grinding), *cazuelas* (casseroles), and *ollas* (earthenware pots). In country kitchens, these tools may still be in use; but in the fine kitchens of the city, they are primarily decorative. In today's modern Mexican kitchen a blender or food processor is standard equipment.

Some of the traditional tools still serve a purpose, however. Although the metate and mano have been largely outmoded by store-bought masa, they are still used to "silken" the masa just before it's balled and patted out or flattened in the tortilla press, and they are often more convenient for grinding nuts and puréeing tomatoes than is the blender sitting beside them. In many kitchens the metate sits on a ledge about a foot below counter height so that the masa maker can get her back into her work. If you are serious about Mexican cooking, you may find a tortilla press indispensable, and you may prefer a good molcajete (after you have ground away all the loose grit) to your mortar and pestle.

Cooking Methods and Secrets

The cooking methods of the Mexican kitchen are not difficult; they are for the most part simple and straightforward. However, they do differ in some ways from the cooking techniques used in the United States.

The cuisine of Mexico is truly colorful, with hearty flavors and savory aromas. Understanding how to use chiles and masa in the appropriate manner is essential. So too is learning the technique for preparing the succulent shredded meats. As you review the recipes in this book you will begin to appreciate these aspects of the cooking of Mexico and your skill in preparing this cuisine will sharpen.

Careful attention is paid to the preparation of the food in Mexico. The freshest ingredients are used, and painstaking (often lengthy) preparation is taken to ensure that the texture and flavor of each ingredient is at its best for the final dish. Often each ingredient is individually toasted or sautéed before being combined or assembled into the final dish. This cooking process defines and enhances the flavor of the ingredient and brings out subtle, underlying flavors that would otherwise be missed.

Nuts or seeds (used as the thickening agents for many of the cooking sauces) are toasted before being finely ground and added to the recipe. Purées are prepared as the base for many sauces or dishes and are sautéed to maximize their flavor before they are combined with the other ingredients. Flour used to thicken some cooking sauces is carefully toasted in oil before the other ingredients are added, eliminating an undesirable raw taste. For some recipes whole (unpeeled) garlic cloves might be toasted on an ungreased *comal* (griddle) or heavy frying pan and then peeled and added to the recipe, providing the full flavor of the garlic but eliminating any raw bite to the taste. In other recipes garlic is peeled and the whole clove is added to oil as it heats; when the garlic is toasted golden, it is removed and discarded. The oil is left with a subtle garlic flavor that is particularly nice in fish and rice dishes.

Seasoning

Herbs and spices are used with a careful hand in authentic Mexican cooking. Seasoning in Mexico is used to enhance the natural flavors of the ingredients rather than as a flavor in itself. For example, a typical combination of spices used in many of the meat dishes and some red cooking sauces is a trio of dried oregano, ground cumin, and ground cloves. The classically balanced ratio is twice as much oregano as cumin and twice as much cumin as cloves (1 teaspoon oregano, ½ teaspoon cumin, ¼ teaspoon cloves). This balance prevents any one seasoning from overpowering the others.

All too often cumin is overused in the preparation of Mexican food in the United States, and the strong flavor of the cumin completely overpowers the taste of the other ingredients. Keep your use of cumin authentic; it's better to use too little than too much. Cumin is used in many meat dishes (shredded fillings and stews) and in some cooking sauces, but it should *not* be used in guacamole, salsas, rice or bean side dishes, and especially *not* with fish or chicken.

Lard Versus Oil

The introduction of the pig to Mexico signaled the only truly basic change in the ancient cooking system. The use of lard provided a new cooking technique. Lard is still the preferred cooking fat in Mexico. For some recipes there can be no substitute for lard and in others the use of lard is optional; however, the final dish may lose a certain "ethnic" flavor dimension if you use oil instead of lard. You will find these recipes specified. For most of the recipes in this book, oil can be used rather than lard without compromising the authentic quality. In many instances, in fact, oil is preferred.

It is important to note that oil used for frying should be heated to the proper temperature for the specific recipe. If it is not, the food will absorb oil during cooking and become greasy, affecting the taste, texture, and overall quality of the food. Use a thermometer to ensure accuracy.

SPECIALTY INGREDIENTS

Most of the ingredients you will need to make the recipes in this book are probably familiar to you, but some are used so differently that it may be a good idea to reintroduce them to you. There are a few ingredients that you are likely to find only in Latin American groceries, but you can grow a number of them in your garden.

Achiote
Annatto seed

Achiote is Spanish for the seed of the annatto tree (*Bixa orellana*). The deep red-orange seeds are used for the brilliant yellow color they impart to food, as well as for their subtle flavor. The dried seeds are cooked in lard or oil until the lard is well colored, then the seeds are removed. A powder, made from the seeds, is used for tinting many things, including butter. In Yucatán, achiote seeds are ground into a paste and used as a base to season meat and fish. The seeds can be found in markets specializing in Latin American foods.

Aguacate
Avocado

There are several varieties of avocado, but you'll probably find either the large, smooth-skinned green ones or the smaller, bumpy-skinned, black Haas variety in your market. The black Haas avocados are the best, but they are available only in the summer. In the winter a number of different smooth-skinned varieties are available; the Fuerte is excellent, but most of the others are watery and flavorless. The Fuerte can be distinguished from these less desirable avocados by its less glossy appearance. Avocados ripen quickly—within two or three days—in a warm kitchen or on a sunny windowsill. Properly ripe avocados should be soft but not mushy, and the seed shouldn't rattle when you shake the fruit. The texture of the flesh should be firm and buttery.

Avocado leaves can be used fresh or dried, ground or whole. They are usually toasted lightly first to bring out the flavor. To determine how strong the flavor of a leaf is, crumble it roughly in your hand or grind it to a powder. It should have a slight licorice aroma.

Canela
Cinnamon

Both true cinnamon bark and cassia bark are sold as cinnamon in the United States. True cinnamon is more delicate in flavor and generally sold in thin quills. In powdered form, true cinnamon is more of a tan color, compared to the reddish brown color of cassia.

Cebollas
Onions

Find a white onion variety with a good, sharp bite to it. White onions are very important for salads, table salsas, and fish recipes. You can substitute yellow onions in other dishes, but in general, yellow onions are too sweet. Purple onions are served pickled and as garnish for antojitos, but they don't have the necessary bite when cooked.

Chayote
Vegetable pear or christophine

This member of the squash family is unlike any other in appearance, texture, or taste. Its subtle texture has made it popular in Chinese cooking, so it is almost always available in Chinese as well as Latin markets; it is also becoming increasingly available in other markets.

The chayote is an elegant vegetable. Its flesh has a reticulated texture like a pear or a watermelon, only much more delicate. The flavor is a bit like cucumber, but much more subtle. Large chayotes should be cut in half or quartered before cooking, and the edible seed should be cut and cooked with it. The chayote is best appreciated in simple form: boiled, peeled, and served hot with butter, or cold in a salad. See additional information on chayote on page 40.

Chiles

See Chiles, Salsas, and Condiments, Chapter 2.

Chorizo
Sausage

Chorizo is a highly seasoned, coarsely ground pork sausage, usually in links. The Mexican *chorizo* is made with fresh pork; the Spanish version is smoked. Always remove the casing before cooking and break the sausage meat apart slightly. It must be cooked thoroughly. To make your own chorizo, see page 88.

Cilantro
Fresh coriander, Chinese parsley

Fresh coriander is called *cilantro* by the Mexicans, *cilantrillo* by Puerto Ricans, and Chinese parsley by many Americans. In Mexican cooking, the fresh leaves of the plant are used. Cilantro has a very distinctive flavor that complements chiles. It should be used carefully until you find out how well you like it. Don't try to substitute the easily available coriander seeds for cilantro; the flavors are entirely different. If ground coriander seed is called for, it is specified as such in the recipes in this book.

Buy cilantro with the roots still on at Oriental or Mexican markets if your local supermarket doesn't have it. To store, place a bunch, unwashed, in a glass of water to cover the roots and cover with a plastic bag. Wash it just before you use it. It doesn't freeze well.

Epazote
Chenopodium, lamb's quarters

The *epazote* of central Mexico has an odor that takes getting used to. It is considered a must for flavoring black beans and is used with a number of other foods. *Chenopodiums* were once cultivated plants and may now be found wild in much of the country. They are generally identified as lamb's quarters and are less strong

in flavor than the Mexican epazote. The strong Mexican variety is *Chenopodium ambrosioides*; the common milder ones are probably *C. fremontii* or *C. album*. Besides being nutritious greens, epazotes are known as carminatives and are used to reduce the gas associated with beans. (A number of other Mexican herbs and spices are said to be carminatives also: oregano, mint, cumin, rosemary, anise, and, of course, chiles.)

Frijoles
Beans

See page 53 in the Salads and Vegetables chapter.

Tomatillos, red beans, avocados, chayotes, nopales, fresh and dried chiles, fava beans, and corn are just some of the ingredients that make the flavors and textures of Mexican food so special.

Cilantro, cinnamon, chocolate, nuts and seeds, ground and whole dried chiles, cumin, oregano and other dried herbs are some of the ingredients essential to making authentic Mexican food.

Hojas
Corn husks

Corn husks are the traditional wrapping for tamales. They're available dried and packaged in Mexican markets and in the specialty section of supermarkets. Trim the ends, flatten them, and they are ready to use. If you get them in their natural state, cut off the butt end to make them straight and even. To soften corn husks, put them in a deep pan, pour very hot water over them, and allow them to soak for several hours. When you're ready to use them, drain or shake to get rid of excess water, and pat them dry with paper towels. They'll be flexible enough to wrap and tie for the tamales.

Jicama
Root vegetable

Jicama is a sweet, brown, round root vegetable, white on the inside. It has a crisp texture, rather like water chestnuts, that is retained even after cooking. It is used in salads and vegetable dishes and is increasingly available in American markets. Jicama is peeled and then washed. Use it raw or sauté it lightly.

Lard
Cooking fat

See page 10 of this chapter.

Maiz and Masa
Corn

See Masa Dishes, pages 56 to 77.

Nopales
Cactus sections

These are the thick, elliptical pads or "leaves" of several varieties of prickly pear cactus (*Opuntia*). If you can find them fresh, choose the smallest, thinnest, palest ones—they'll be the most tender and the best flavored. Some species of *Opuntia* are spineless; if you get the thorny kind, you'll have to scrape the spines from the sides and edges (use tongs to handle; the spines are nasty). Leave as much of the green skin as possible. Cut into small pieces and cook until tender in well-salted water.

Cooked nopales may have a slippery quality somewhat like okra, but there are several ways to minimize this. One method is to rinse the cooked nopales, drain them in a colander, cover with a damp towel to keep them from drying out, and let them stand for about 30 minutes. Another way is to cook diced nopales in an ungreased pan with several chunks of onion and a clove or two of garlic until the nopales are no longer slippery (about 5 minutes). Rinse in a colander, then proceed with the recipe.

If you can't find fresh ones, canned nopales are a good substitute.

Nueces y Semillas
Nuts and seeds

Peanuts, pecans, and pumpkin seeds (*pepitas*) are all native to Mexico. They are ground very fine and are often used instead of flour, egg yolks, or cream to thicken sauces. (If your recipe calls for pumpkin seeds, look for shelled, unsalted ones in health food stores or specialty shops.)

The Spanish introduced almonds, filberts, walnuts, pine nuts, and sesame seeds, and all are widely used throughout Mexico and are readily available in the United States.

Oregano
Fresh or dried herbs

In Mexico there are many different plants called oregano. The favored Mexican oregano is a small shrub of the *Verbena* family. It is more aromatic and pungent than the *Origanum* used in the United States.

Piloncillo
Raw sugar cones

Piloncillo is Mexican raw sugar sold in very small to very large cones. Dark brown sugar may be substituted.

Plátano
Plantains, cooking bananas

Plantains are a large banana variety that must be cooked to be edible. They must also be ripe to be peeled; ripe ones are black and soft. The most common way to cook plantains is to slice them lengthwise ½ inch thick and fry them in oil. Another way is to slice them into thin rounds and fry until crisp—they taste like potato chips, but sweet. Regular green, firm bananas will substitute, but they need less cooking time.

Queso
Cheese

Since the Spanish introduction of cows and goats in the sixteenth century, cheese has become an integral element of Mexican cooking.

Besides adding distinctive tastes and textures to dishes, cheese contains nearly all the fat, casein, calcium, and vitamin A that was in the milk. Cheese is about 25 percent casein, a valuable protein that constitutes only 3 percent of whole milk. As an important bonus, cheese nicely complements the relatively incomplete proteins found in beans and corn, making them nutritionally more valuable.

Good Mexican cheeses are rarely available in the United States. If you have no luck at Mexican markets, and you're the do-it-yourself type, try making your own cheeses or try the following substitutions.

Queso anejo is sharp and salty; excellent for filling enchiladas. Try using Gruyère as a substitute.

Queso asadero is a mild cheese, thinly sliced and packaged like tortillas. Substitute provolone or mozzarella.

Queso Chihuahua is sharp, but softer and less salty than *queso anejo*. Substitute medium Cheddar, Parmesan, or Romano.

Queso fresco is a fresh, unripened, perishable cheese. Substitute dry cottage cheese or Italian ricotta cheese. If these seem too mild, try mixing them with a little Greek feta cheese, or make your own whey cheese.

Queso de Oaxaca is stringy and slightly tart. Substitute jack cheese.

Queso panela is a mild cheese aged in baskets and therefore readily identified by the woven imprint on the rind. Substitute jack cheese.

Tomate, jitomate
Tomatoes

Unfortunately, American tomatoes have been bred for their shipping qualities at the expense of flavor. If such tomatoes are all that's available, opt for canned ones. For best flavor, grow your own.

Tomatoes are often *asado* (roasted) in Mexican recipes. This is traditionally done on the comal, but it's messy. It's easier to line a shallow pan with aluminum foil and slip the tomatoes under the broiler. A medium-sized tomato will take about 20 minutes. Turn to cook evenly. The skin may be removed before broiling or left on, but the charred skin adds flavor. Blend into a fairly smooth sauce.

To peel tomatoes, dip them in boiling water for a minute or two. The skin will slip off easily.

Tomatillo
Also called tomate de cascara

There are a number of similar plants in this group that are often seen in Mexican markets. They vary from the size of a large pea to the size of a golf ball. The smaller varieties resemble our husk tomato (ground cherry, or Cape gooseberry), but the real tomatillo (*Physalis ixocarpa*) generally fills the paper-like husk, rather than hanging within it as most of the others do.

This vegetable does not develop its flavor until cooked. The flavor of the tomatillo is subtle and distinctive, resembling a tomato with a touch of lemon. Cooked tomatillos are available canned, called *tomatillos entero* or *tomate verde*.

Below are two basic cooking methods for preparing fresh tomatillos.

1. Remove the husk and rinse the tomatillos. Place in a saucepan and cover with cold water. Bring to a boil and cook over low heat until transparent (approximately 5 minutes). Drain, to use immediately; store in the refrigerator or freezer in their own liquid for later use.

2. Preheat a comal or heavy frying pan over medium heat. Place the tomatillos on the comal with their husks on. Toast gently, turning often, until the tomatillo flesh is soft and the husk quite brown (approximately 10 minutes). Remove husk.

Chiles are the central ingredient in Mexican cuisine. An astounding variety of chiles is available, and the subtle differences in their flavors are fascinating.

Chiles, Salsas & Condiments

The chile plays a major role in Mexican cooking. It is a vegetable that seems to have an infinite number of varieties with just as many different uses. Chiles are used in sauces, salsas, with vegetables, in salads, in masa dishes, with meats, seafood, and poultry, and in drinks. Here we discuss how to identify chiles, how to use them, and how to make the most of their varied flavors. Jalapeño, poblano, serrano, ancho, pasilla, and pequin are a few of the most common chiles; they will be your starting point for preparing authentic Mexican dishes.

THE IMPORTANCE OF THE CHILE

Although knowing how to use chiles is the key to creating delicious Mexican foods, don't be confused or intimidated by the variety and versatility of chiles. You will need to be familiar with only a few of the most commonly used chiles to make most of the recipes in this book.

The chile is a member of the genus *Capsicum* and is unrelated to the *Piper* family from which we get black pepper. Although the hot spiciness of each may imply a relationship, botanically they are quite different.

Chiles fall into two basic categories: cooking chiles and garnish or condiment chiles. Cooking chiles, used in such main dishes as moles, adobos, and chiles rellenos, and as a basis for cooking sauces, generally are not hot. (With few exceptions, Mexican main dishes are mild enough to suit almost any palate.) On the other hand, garnish or condiment chiles, pickled or used in table salsas, *are* hot.

A beginning Mexican cook will want to know which chiles are hot and which are mild. On page 18 chiles are divided into hot and mild groups, but you will discover that you have to taste each chile to find your preference.

Part of the difficulty in determining the flavor of certain chiles is that there are many varieties (probably over a hundred in Mexico), and all of these cross-pollinate with great ease. As if this weren't enough, a chile that is mild when grown in the favorable conditions of a California coastal valley will become hot when grown in the harsher, more stressful conditions of New Mexico.

The bright red and yellow colors of ripe chiles are due to the content of capsanthin and various other carotenoids, including carotene. The "hot" or pungent substance in chiles is called capsaicin. It is concentrated in the central ribs and veins where the seeds attach, and, contrary to common belief, it is the veins that are hot, not the seeds.

The effect of chiles on the digestion is likely to play a major part in any spirited chile discussion. Very early medical literature in western Europe ascribed rather miraculous efficacy to the chile. It was touted as a cure for everything from dropsy, colic, and diarrhea to toothache and constipation.

During the early years of scientific nutritional research in the United States, the chile was firmly condemned as nothing more than a means of concealing the flavor of rotten meat. In 1924, a book on Mexico concluded, "The most detrimental factor in the (Mexican) diet is the caustic chile." More recent research has shown that the chile does, indeed, have certain medicinal attributes. We now know that the chile, as an aid to digestion, increases salivation to as much as eight times above the normal resting rate. Taken internally, chiles can raise body temperature and act as a general stimulant. Externally, they act as a counter-irritant for relief of muscular pain.

A significant recent finding at New Mexico State University suggests that the early Indians knew what they were doing when they coated their meats with chile pulp. Studies show that chile is an antioxidant and when included in meat dishes it retards the oxidation of fats, delays rancidity, and contributes to significantly longer storage life.

In Mexico a chile may get its name from its use, such as *chile para relleno* "for stuffing" or *huachinango* "cooked with red snapper"; from a region, such as Tabasco; from its shape, such as *ancho* (broad); or from its color, *guero* (blond) or *colorado* (red). In most cases, the name of the chile changes when it is dried. In addition, the name *pasilla* is confusingly applied to six or seven different dried *or* fresh chiles, most of them mild. Dr. Roy Nakayama (known as the "Doctor of Hot" among some chile aficionados) of the New Mexico State University horticulture department tells of ordering pasillas from as many different sources as he could find and planting their seeds. The pasillas that he raised varied from long and slender to full and broad.

Dr. Nakayama and his associates also developed the New Mexico 6-4, mildest of the New Mexico chiles and, more recently, the hotter Mex Big Jim. The prolific Mex Big Jim matures early and produces chiles up to 12 inches long.

Chipotles and jalapeños also contribute to the confusing chile nomenclature. The name *chipotle* comes from the Nahuatl words *chil* (chile) and *poctli* (smoke) and most authorities agree that the chipotle is a smoked jalapeño chile. Our confidence in this definition was shaken by a statement in one Spanish-language book that "the dried *cuaresmeno* chile is called *chipotle*." Subsequently we have found references to chipotles as "yellow chiles in vinegar" and a recipe calling for "fresh chipotles"—certainly a contradiction in terms.

Actually, we could dismiss the cuaresmeno, or Lenten, chile, as simply another name for the jalapeño—although there are those who insist that these are distinct chiles. In Vera Cruz, however, the jalapeño has still another name—the huachinango, presumably because it is used in cooking the fish of that name. Or could it be named after the town of Huachinango? It seems fitting that in the town of Huachinango two distinctly different smoked chiles are being sold side by side as chipotles. We still think chipotles are smoked jalapeños.

HOW CHILES ARE USED

Cooking Chiles

Cooking chiles, such as poblanos and anaheims, are used either fresh or canned. Canned chiles are generally roasted and peeled before canning, and can be substituted for fresh chiles.

To Roast, Peel, and Seed Fresh Chiles

Roasting chiles loosens their skin, making them easier to peel. You can roast chiles over a gas flame, on an electric burner, under a broiler, or you can deep-fry them in hot oil. Chiles roasted over a burner or in a broiler will char a bit; this gives them a better flavor than deep-fried chiles. However too much roasting can cause the chile's flesh to become bitter. Deep-frying is best when you have a large number of chiles to prepare, or when you want the chile to be especially crisp.

To roast chiles, spear them with a large fork or long skewer then place them over an open flame or electric burner or under a broiler until the skins are blistered and charred.

To deep-fry chiles, preheat oil—deep enough to cover the chiles—to 400° F. Add a few chiles to the oil and fry until they are blistered. Adding too many chiles at once will cause them to cook too slowly, and they will absorb oil.

After roasting or deep-frying, either wrap them in a damp towel or place them in a tightly closed plastic bag for 20 minutes to steam them. This will cause the chile to go limp. If you want crisp chiles, plunge them into ice water immediately after roasting or deep-frying.

When chiles are cool, remove the skin under running water, beginning at the stem end. Slit the chile open and gently scrape out the veins and seeds.

Garnish Chiles

The garnish chiles are used fresh or pickled (*en escabeche*), in table salsas or as garnishes. They are not roasted or peeled. The stem is always removed, but removing the seeds is optional. You may remove the veins in order to make them less hot. In a cooked salsa, garnish chiles are simmered with other ingredients. Jalapeño, serrano, and guero are among the most commonly used garnish chiles.

Whole Dried Chiles

Dried chiles are used in two ways: either as chile pulp for purée or a dry powder. Traditionally chiles are sun-dried, but many are now being dried in ovens. This can cause the skin to become bitter, so it is best to roast the dried chiles as illustrated, then soak them in cold water for 30 minutes and then remove the skin.

Chile Pulp To prepare chile pulp, remove stems and seeds, open the chiles flat, and place them in a saucepan. Use a small plate to weight them down, and add water to cover. Bring to a boil, reduce heat to medium, and cook for 5 minutes. Set aside for 30 minutes to steep. Drain the chiles (reserving the liquid) and place them in a blender or food processor. Blend briefly to an even purée. For a smooth texture, strain through a sieve to remove larger pieces of skin.

Ground Chile Preheat a comal or heavy frying pan and toast chiles well (about 5 minutes) over medium heat, turning frequently to prevent burning. Allow to cool slightly, break open, and remove stem, seeds, and membrane. Crumble one chile at a time into a molcajete or blender, and grind to a fine powder. (A rotary-bladed coffee grinder works even better than a blender.)

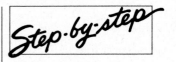

HOW TO ROAST AND PEEL CHILES

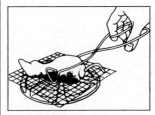

1. *Blister chile pod over a gas or electric burner covered with a metal screen. Turn frequently with tongs. The chiles are done when the skins are charred and blistered. Some parts of the chile will be black. Take care not to burn through to the flesh. Place blistered chiles immediately in a plastic bag to steam for 20 minutes.*

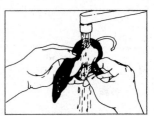

2. *When chiles are cool, hold them under cool water and peel the skin from the chile, starting from the stem end. Wear rubber gloves if you are peeling very many chiles or if you have sensitive skin.*

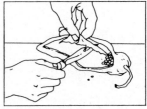

3. *With a small, sharp knife, cut open the chile. Remove the veins and seeds. Wash out the last of the seeds under running water.*

Using Commercial Powdered Chile

We have purposely used the term ground chile, because most products that are simply labeled "chili powder" also contain a number of other ingredients, including cumin, oregano, onion, and garlic. The amount of cumin used in these products will overpower most of the recipes in this book. Pure ground chiles are available in cellophane packages in the Mexican food section of many markets. The unseasoned ground chiles are often labeled "puro." These ground chiles are available from mild and medium to the hot New Mexico. A good powdered chile must be fresh and should be ground without the seeds; stale powder and powder that includes seeds are yellowish in color. The seeds and veins result in a hotter, but relatively less flavorful, powder. Bright, rich color is likely to mean fresh, flavorful powdered chile.

CHILE IDENTIFICATION

Because much of the confusion regarding chiles stems from the fact that the name of a fresh chile often changes when the chile is dried, knowing your chiles will help you avoid any surprises. Generally the smaller the chile the hotter, but there are enough exceptions to get you into trouble if you are not cautious.

The photographs and chart will help you identify the different chiles. Only the most common chiles in their most typical forms (fresh, dried, or both) are pictured.

Certain chiles may be used interchangeably, depending on availability. Once you feel secure with the chiles listed here, you may wish to become adventuresome and substitute others (fresh, canned, dried, or ground) available in your area.

CHILE IDENTIFICATION CHART

Here we describe the many varieties of cooking and garnish chiles. All cooking chiles are more mild than garnish chiles. Garnish chiles might best be described as hot, hotter, and hottest. There are flavor and texture distinctions between the garnish chiles; however, since they are all quite hot, only the most educated palate is likely to fully appreciate the distinctions.

COOKING CHILES—MILD FLAVORED

Fresh: Poblano   Dried: Ancho   Ground: Ancho

This is the cooking chile most commonly used in Mexico. It may be marketed as pasilla in its fresh, dried, or ground forms.

Fresh: Anaheim   Dried: California   Ground: California

This chile may be substituted for the poblano or ancho chile described above; it is the cooking chile most commonly found in the United States. It is easily identified in its fresh or dried form because of its long green shape. It is marketed throughout this country as "whole green chiles" or "diced green chiles," in 4-ounce or 7-ounce cans. This chile is also referred to as "long green chile" or "mild green chile." A New Mexico variety, available fresh, dried, and ground, looks similar to but is much hotter than the more common variety. Fortunately it is identified as "New Mexico."

Fresh: Not available   Dried: Mulato   Ground: Mulato

The fresh mulato is not often used in Mexico and is not available in the United States. The dried mulato is used in some cooking sauces, such as Mole Poblano (see page 90). If it is not available in your area, substitute ancho.

Fresh: Not available   Dried: Pasilla   Ground: Pasilla

The fresh pasilla is not often used in Mexico and is not available in the United States. You may find the fresh poblano and the dried ancho marketed as pasilla chiles. To confuse matters even more, you may also find the pasilla chile marketed as "chile negro." The pasilla is one of the hotter cooking chiles. It is used sparingly and in combination with other chiles for an added "zap" in certain recipes.

GARNISH CHILES

Fresh: Jalapeño   Canned: Jalapeño   Dried: Chipotle

Hot—This is the most widely available garnish chile (fresh or canned) in Mexico. The chipotle is a smoke-dried jalapeño with a wonderful flavor. The chipotle is generally not available in the United States; be sure to try it if you can find it.

Fresh and Canned: Guero (Wax) and Fresno   Dried: Guero and Fresno

Hot—Although these chiles are two distinct varieties, they are similar in flavor characteristics and heat level and may be used interchangeably.

Fresh: Serrano   Canned: Serrano   Dried: Serrano seco, Japonés, and chile de Arbol

Hotter—The serrano may be found fresh, canned, or dried. Although the dried Japonés and chile de Arbol are distinct varieties, they are similar in flavor and heat level and to the dried serrano and may be used interchangeably.

Dried: Cascabel

Hot—The dried chile cascabel is not always available in the United States, but it has a wonderful nutlike flavor. Be sure to try it if you can find it.

Dried: Tepin and pequin

Hottest—The tepin is a very small round chile and the pequin is a very small oval chile. Both are quite fiery. Use sparingly.

DRIED CHILES

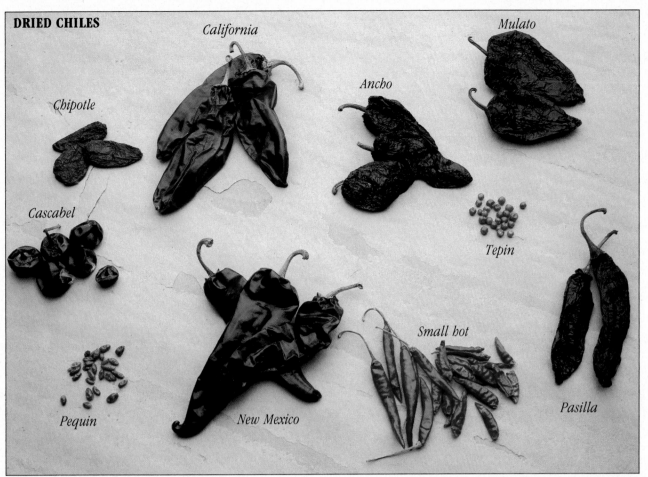

California

Mulato

Chipotle

Ancho

Cascabel

Tepin

Pequin

New Mexico

Small hot

Pasilla

FRESH CHILES

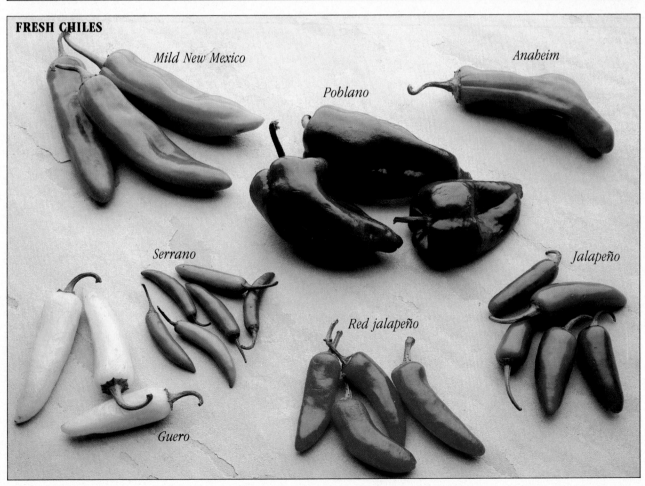

Mild New Mexico

Anaheim

Poblano

Serrano

Jalapeño

Red jalapeño

Guero

HOW TO STORE AND PRESERVE CHILES

Chiles can be canned, pickled, frozen, and, of course, dried. The availability of good fresh chiles varies seasonally, even in markets that specialize in Mexican ingredients. For instructions for canning chiles, see page 24.

To Refrigerate Fresh Chiles

Store chiles, loosely wrapped, in refrigerator. Cooking chiles—poblano, anaheim, and fresh New Mexico chiles—should be used within three days for maximum flavor. They keep for up to a week but will gradually shrivel and lose their flavor. Garnish chiles, such as jalapeños and serranos, will keep in the refrigerator for up to three weeks.

To Freeze Fresh Chiles

Cooking chiles are roasted and peeled before freezing. See page 17 for instructions. When the chiles are cool, seed and devein them. Wrap them individually in plastic bags or waxed paper, then pack all the chiles in a plastic freezer bag. Another method, convenient if you want to have diced chiles on hand, is to bunch the peeled and cleaned chiles together, wrap, and freeze them. Shave off as much as you need whenever a recipe calls for diced chiles.

To freeze fresh garnish chiles, first cook them for a few minutes in a dry skillet or boil them in a little water.

To Store Dried Chiles

Under cool, dry conditions dried chiles, packed in tightly sealed jars, will keep well through one season's storage (if moisture condenses in the jar, the chiles are not dry enough). Dried chiles may also be ground and stored in tightly sealed jars. However, if you have room, the best place to store whole or ground dried chiles is in tightly closed plastic bags in the freezer.

Substitutions

You may sometimes have to substitute canned mild green chiles for fresh mild chiles and you may have to use commercial powdered chiles instead of chile pulp from dried chiles. One tablespoon of powdered chiles is about equal to one dried ancho, California, or pasilla chile.

The commonly available seasoned chili powder can be used if nothing else is available. It contains paprika, oregano, cumin, garlic powder, and other spices. Using these powders successfully will require adjustment in the amounts of the additional spices that might also be listed in the recipe; of course, they might include seasonings you don't want.

Cayenne pepper or ground red pepper may be used as a substitute for pequin, tepin, and the other small, hot dried chiles.

Fresh cayenne chiles, along with various other fresh chiles such as Japanese, Hontakas, and Louisiana hots, are often available in our markets and may, in their green stage, be substituted for the Mexican garnish chiles.

You can use the grated inside pulp of bell pepper to augment the flavor of canned green chiles and to dilute the heat of some fresh green chiles. This combination achieves a flavor close to the fresh poblano, the most popular mild cooking chile in Mexico. It is important, however, not to let the bell pepper flavor overpower the more subtle flavor of the green chile.

It is also possible to use grated bell pepper with a few drops of Tabasco when there are no fresh chiles available.

A Word of Caution

Chiles can burn the skin. Some people are more sensitive than others. The potency can be deceptive because there is a delayed reaction between contact and sensation. When handling chiles, keep your hands away from your face, especially your eyes. When finished, wash your hands thoroughly with soap and water.

The hottest part of a chile is the placental tissue that connects the seed to the walls, so cleaning chiles exposes you more than do other operations. If you are going to handle many chiles or if you have tender skin, wear rubber gloves.

Soaking green chiles in cold water with a little salt or vinegar will remove some of the heat from them. Soaking them much longer than 30 minutes will begin to remove the flavor as well as the heat.

SAUCES VERSUS SALSAS

An important distinction needs to be made regarding the words *sauce* and *salsa* as used in the Mexican cuisine.

Salsa literally translates as "sauce," but Mexicans and Mexican cookbooks use the word *salsa* only to refer to the table salsas that are served as garnishes and condiments. Sauces used in cooking, on the other hand, are never referred to as salsas. Each cooking sauce is specifically named; sometimes for its region of origin, or for the type of chile used, for its color, or even for the recipe in which it is used.

Cooking Sauces

These wonderful sauces are an integral part of the Mexican cuisine. They feature just the right combination of chiles and other ingredients. The chiles are made into a purée on which the sauce will be based. This purée is carefully seasoned, then ground nuts or seeds are added to thicken the sauce as it cooks.

Flour is used as a thickening agent only in Northern Mexico, the wheat-growing region. (Cornstarch is sometimes used in the United States as a thickening agent for some of the green cooking sauces; it is not used in the authentic cuisine.) The purée is then sautéed, and broth is slowly stirred in until the desired consistency is achieved. These cooking sauces have a wonderful flavor and texture. The recipes for the cooking sauces will be found with the meat, poultry and fish recipes they accompany.

Salsas

The Mexican table setting is incomplete without its bowl of chile salsa. In fact in many homes and restaurants more than one salsa will be available, one milder than the other. Salsas typically have a high heat level and they are served as a garnish or condiment to be applied individually to personal taste. There are fresh salsas, cooked salsas, red ones and green ones, and the type of chile and the quantity used will determine how hot the salsa will be. The ingredients common to most salsas are onions, garlic, tomatoes (for the red salsas) or tomatillos (for the green salsas), fresh cilantro, and, of course, chiles. The chiles used for salsas are the garnish chiles and they may be used fresh, dried, or ground.

A nice way to prepare the garlic for salsas, particularly the uncooked salsas, is to toast unpeeled garlic cloves on an ungreased comal until soft. Peel the garlic, mash it into a purée, then proceed with the recipe. This method is often used in Mexico and provides the full flavor of the garlic without adding a raw "bite" to the taste.

FRESH SALSAS

SALSA CRUDA
Fresh salsa

This is a mild table salsa using fresh chopped ingredients, yielding a pleasant chunky texture. It is indispensable on the Mexican table and is served with almost every meal. Usually there would be a second salsa on the table having a smoother puréed texture and hot taste, providing a choice of heat level and texture.

- 2 mild, long green chiles, chopped or 1 can (4 oz) diced green chiles
- 2 large tomatoes, chopped Half a small white onion, minced, or 2 green onions, chopped
- 1 tablespoon vinegar
- 1 clove garlic, minced
- 2 tablespoons cilantro leaves Salt to taste (optional)

In a medium bowl mix together chiles, tomatoes, onion, vinegar, garlic, and cilantro. Add salt to taste, if desired, and serve in a bowl as a condiment.

Makes 2½ cups.

SALSA DE CHILE ROJO
Red chile salsa

This salsa has a wonderful hot and garlicky bite. It is an excellent dipping sauce for seafood.

- 3 dried ancho chiles
- 2 dried pasilla chiles
- 3 large whole tomatoes
- 3 cloves garlic, chopped
- ½ teaspoon salt
- ¼ teaspoon dried oregano
- 3 green onions, finely chopped

1. Remove stems and most of the seeds from chiles. Open chiles flat, place in a saucepan, and weight them down with a plate. Barely cover chiles with water, bring to a boil, and cook for 5 minutes over medium heat. Set aside at least 30 minutes to steep.

2. Broil tomatoes, turning several times, until soft and cooked through (about 15 minutes).

3. Drain chiles and place in a blender or food processor with garlic, tomatoes, salt, and oregano. Blend briefly to an even consistency. Stir in the chopped onions.

Makes about 3 cups.

SALSA DE CHILE JAPONÉS
Japonés chile salsa

This is a hot table salsa with a garlicky flavor. If you wish to take the edge off the garlic taste, toast the unpeeled clove of garlic on a comal or in a heavy skillet, turning until the peel is lightly browned; then peel, chop, and add it to the blender. For a milder salsa add 1 to 2 tomatoes or decrease the number of chiles. For a thinner salsa, add small amounts of water when blending until it reaches the desired consistency.

- 4 Japonés chiles
- 2 large tomatoes, peeled and cut into chunks
- 2 tablespoons minced white onion or 1 green onion, chopped
- 1 to 2 cloves garlic, minced
- 1 tablespoon cilantro leaves Salt to taste

1. Toast the Japonés chiles on a comal or in a heavy skillet, turning until slightly crisp but not browned. Crumble the chiles into a blender and finely blend.

2. Add tomatoes, onion, and garlic and blend to a smooth purée. Pour into a bowl and stir in cilantro and salt.

Makes about 1 cup.

SALSA AZTECA
A hot table salsa

This is a hot, somewhat chunky table salsa. For a smoother texture, place the ingredients in a blender or food processor and blend briefly to a smooth purée. If a milder salsa is desired, substitute canned diced green chiles for the jalapeño or serrano chiles.

- 3 jalapeño or 4 serrano chiles, fresh or canned, minced
- 5 large tomatoes, peeled and finely chopped
- 2 cloves garlic, minced
- 1 small white onion, minced
- 1 tablespoon vinegar
- 2 tablespoons chopped cilantro
  Salt to taste

In a medium bowl mix together chiles, tomatoes, garlic, onion, and vinegar. Stir in the cilantro and salt.

Makes 4 cups.

SALSA VERDE
Green salsa

This green salsa has an unusually fresh flavor that results from the blending of tomatillos and cilantro. It is particularly good with pork, chicken, and fish dishes.

- 1 jalapeño or 2 serrano chiles, fresh or canned, chopped
- 1 can (12 oz) tomatillos, drained or 8 fresh tomatillos, cooked and drained (see page 13 for cooking instructions)
- 2 cloves garlic, chopped
- 3 tablespoons finely minced white onion or 2 green onions, finely chopped
- ¼ cup cilantro leaves
- ¼ teaspoon salt
- ¼ cup water

1. Place chiles, tomatillos, garlic, onion, cilantro, and salt in a blender or food processor and blend briefly to a purée.

2. Add the water in small amounts and blend to the desired consistency.

Makes about 1½ cups.

SALSA DE CHIPOTLE
Chipotle chile salsa

This is a hot table salsa that has a wonderful smoky flavor, the result of the smoke-dried chiles. As with Salsa Verde, this table salsa is particularly good with pork, chicken, and fish dishes.

- 3 or 4 chipotle chiles
- 1 can (12 oz) tomatillos, drained, or 9 fresh tomatillos, cooked and drained (see page 13)
- 2 cloves garlic, chopped (see Note)
- 3 tablespoons finely minced white onion or 2 green onions, finely minced
- ¼ cup coarsely chopped cilantro
- ¼ cup water

1. Toast the chiles on a comal or in a heavy skillet, turning until they are slightly crisp and lightly browned. Remove the stems and crumble the chiles into a blender. Grind the chiles until fine.

2. Add tomatillos, garlic, onion, and cilantro and blend briefly to a purée. Add the water in small amounts and blend to the desired consistency.

Makes about 1½ cups.

Note If you wish to take the edge off the garlic, toast the unpeeled cloves on a comal or heavy skillet, turning until the peel is lightly browned. Peel, chop, and add to the blender.

COOKED SALSAS

Cooked salsas are less piquant and more saucelike than their fresh counterparts. Their degree of hotness depends on the chiles used. They can be stored in the refrigerator for three to four days, or can be frozen.

SALSA DE JALAPEÑOS ROJOS
Red jalapeño cooked salsa

Occasionally you may be fortunate enough to find fresh red jalapeño chiles in your local market. If you do, by all means try this wonderful cooked salsa. It is particularly nice served with vegetables, fish, or eggs. If you grow your own jalapeños, allow some of them to turn red for use in this unique salsa.

- 3 large tomatoes
  Half an onion, chopped
- ½ teaspoon salt
- 2 tablespoons oil
- 4 cloves garlic
- 4 fresh red jalapeño chiles, roasted, peeled, cleaned, and cut into rajas (strips)
- 1 sprig epazote or 2 tablespoons coarsely chopped cilantro (optional)

1. Broil tomatoes until fork-tender (about 10 minutes) and peel. Place tomatoes, onion, and salt in a blender or food processor and whirl briefly to an even consistency.

2. In a skillet heat oil. Add garlic, and toast to a golden brown. Remove garlic and discard. Add the chiles and sauté briefly over high heat.

3. Add the tomato mixture and epazote (if used) and cook over medium high heat, stirring, until the sauce thickens, approximately 8 to 12 minutes. Serve warm.

Makes about 3 cups.

SALSA FRITA
Cooked salsa

This is a zesty, all-purpose salsa. If a milder salsa is desired, substitute 1 can (4 oz) diced green chiles for the jalapeño chiles.

  *Half a small white
  onion, minced*
 1 clove garlic, minced or pressed
 1 tablespoon oil
 *2 fresh or canned
  jalapeño chiles, seeded
  and chopped*
 *2 large tomatoes, peeled
  and chopped
  Salt to taste*
 *1 tablespoon chopped cilantro
  or pinch dried oregano*

1. In a skillet sauté onion and garlic in oil until soft. Add chiles and tomatoes and simmer for 15 minutes.

2. Check the seasoning and add salt to taste. Stir in cilantro.

Makes 2 cups.

SALSA VERDE FRITA
Cooked green salsa

This is particularly good with pork, chicken, and fish dishes. If a milder salsa is desired, subsitute 1 can (4 oz) diced green chiles in place of the jalapeño or serrano chiles.

 *1 can (12 oz) tomatillos,
  drained, or 9 fresh tomatillos,
  cooked and drained*
 *1 jalapeño or 2 serrano chiles,
  fresh or canned, chopped
  Half a white onion, chopped*
 1 clove garlic, minced
 ¼ cup cilantro leaves
 *2 tablespoons oil
  Salt to taste*

1. Place tomatillos, chiles, onion, garlic, and cilantro in a blender or food processor and whirl briefly to purée.

2. In a skillet heat oil and sauté the purée, stirring constantly, for 2 or 3 minutes. Check the seasoning and add salt to taste. Serve hot or cold as a table salsa.

Makes 1½ cups.

A Mexican table setting is incomplete without a bowl of chile salsa. The range of red and green salsas and their degrees of hotness are almost as extensive as the variety of chiles.

CANNING CHILES AND SALSAS

Canning chiles and salsas is a good way to preserve them for later use and to assure that you will always have plenty of salsa on hand when you prepare Mexican food. For canning, choose ingredients that are firm, fresh, and free from bruises or blemishes. Wash the ingredients thoroughly.

Chiles are a low-acid food and you must carefully follow the proper processing directions for canning them. Do not adjust the recipes or the processing directions. Use distilled white vinegar—with at least a 5 percent acetic acid content. These processing directions are courtesy of University of California, Cooperative Extension, Davis, California.

Read "A Word of Caution," page 20, before you proceed.

DIRECTIONS FOR PROCESSING

The following are general guidelines for canning chiles and salsas. Use them in conjunction with the recipes that follow.

1. Select the canning jars and lids carefully. Do not use jars that are chipped or cracked. Jars must be clean and hot when they are filled. Scald lids before they are used, taking care not to boil them. Follow the manufacturer's directions.

2. Follow the recipe and fill the jars as instructed, leaving the specified amount of headspace. Remove any air bubbles by running a plastic spatula between the food and the jar.

3. Clean the rim and threads of the jar carefully with a clean, damp cloth. This is especially important when oil is used in the recipe.

4. Place the lid on the jar and secure with a ring band. Follow the lid manufacturer's instructions for tightening.

5. Use a deep kettle with a rack placed on the bottom. The kettle must be deep enough for the tops of the jars to be covered with water. Fill the kettle half full of water. Place the jars in the water bath and add enough water to cover the tops of the jars.

6. Use a candy or meat thermometer to determine the temperature of the simmering water bath. Begin to count the processing time when the water bath temperature has reached 170° F. Process for the full time indicated in the recipe.

7. As you remove the jars from the water bath, do not disturb the seal. Leave the ring bands on the jars until they have cooled thoroughly. Place the hot jars, well separated, on a rack or folded towel away from drafts or cool surfaces.

8. When the jars are cool, check the lids to be sure they are sealed. The lid should be concave and should not give when pressed in the center. The ring bands can be removed.

9. Store the jars in a cool, dry, dark place. Storage temperatures should not exceed 75° F. Store opened jars in the refrigerator.

SALSA
Canned salsa

1 pound onions, chopped
6 cloves garlic, minced
2 pounds fresh jalapeño or other hot chile, finely chopped
5 pounds tomatoes, peeled and chopped
2 teaspoons salt
¾ cup vinegar
¼ cup cilantro leaves (optional)

1. Place onion, garlic, chiles, tomatoes, salt, and vinegar in a large pot. Heat to simmering and simmer for 10 minutes. Stir in cilantro.

2. Pack into clean, hot pint or half-pint canning jars. Adjust lids and rings and seal. Allow ½ inch headspace. Follow Directions for Processing (left) and process for 15 minutes in a simmering hot-water bath.

Makes 12 to 16 cups (6 to 8 pints).

JALAPEÑOS EN ESCABECHE
Canned jalapeños

Jalapeño chiles
Carrot slices
Small chunks of onion
½ teaspoon salt per pint
1 clove garlic, minced, per pint
Vinegar and water in equal amounts, to cover the vegetables
Oil

1. Prick or slash the chiles in several places. Pack into clean pint canning jars. Add a few carrot slices and onion pieces. Add salt and garlic.

2. Cover ingredients with equal amounts of vinegar and water, leaving ¾ inch headspace. Top with a thin layer of oil (⅛ inch). Wipe jar rim clean with a damp cloth. Adjust lids and rings. Seal. Follow Directions for Processing (left) and process for 15 minutes in a simmering hot-water bath.

SALSA VERDE
Canned green salsa

5 pounds tomatillos
1 pound onions, chopped
6 cloves garlic, minced
2 pounds fresh jalapeño or other hot chile, finely chopped
2 teaspoons salt
¾ cup vinegar
½ cup finely chopped cilantro

1. Remove husks from tomatillos. Wash the tomatillos thoroughly and place them in a large pot. Cover with cold water, bring to a boil, reduce heat, and simmer until transparent (approximately 5 minutes). Drain. Place in a blender or food processor and blend to an even consistency.

2. Place tomatillo purée, onion, garlic, chiles, salt, and vinegar in a large pot. Heat to simmering and simmer 5 minutes. Stir in cilantro.

3. Pack into clean, hot pint or half-pint canning jars, leaving ½ inch headspace. Adjust lids and rings. Seal. Follow Directions for Processing (opposite page) and process for 15 minutes in a simmering hot-water bath.

Makes 12 to 16 cups (6 to 8 pints).

Note If a milder salsa is desired, use fewer chiles or choose a milder chile, such as the long green anaheim variety.

CONDIMENTS

ESCABECHE DE CEBOLLA
Pickled onions

Pickled onions are one of the most important garnishes for Mexican dishes. Red onions are especially attractive prepared this way.

> 2 *white or red onions, thinly sliced and separated into rings*
> 6 *peppercorns*
> 2 *tablespoons cilantro leaves or ¼ teaspoon dried oregano*
> 3 *cloves garlic, minced*
> ¼ *teaspoon salt Vinegar and water, in equal amounts, to cover the onions (or use rice wine vinegar and do not use water)*

1. Place onions, peppercorns, cilantro, garlic, and salt in a quart jar. Add vinegar and water.

2. Store, covered, in the refrigerator. Make at least 1 day in advance; flavor improves as the onions season. Serve as a garnish or condiment or add to green salad. They will keep for several weeks.

Makes 4 cups.

CEBOLLA EN LIMA
Onions in lime juice

Here is another version of pickled onions.

> 1 *large red onion, thinly sliced and separated into rings Juice from 3 fresh limes*
> 1 *tablespoon cilantro leaves or pinch dried oregano*

1. In a glass bowl place onions in lime juice and stir in cilantro.

2. Cover, refrigerate, and allow to marinate for 3 hours or longer. They will keep several weeks in the refrigerator. Serve as a garnish or condiment or add to a green salad.

Serves 3 to 4.

ZANAHORIA EN ESCABECHE
Marinated carrots

> 3 *carrots, cut into large chunks*
> ½ *cup Oil and Vinegar Dressing (see page 44)*
> 1 *or more tablespoons liquid from canned jalapeños Pinch dried oregano*

1. Briefly steam the carrots until barely fork-tender (3 to 4 minutes). Take care not to overcook. Rinse in cold water and place in a bowl.

2. Combine dressing and jalapeño liquid. Add oregano and pour the dressing over the carrots. Cover and refrigerate to marinate for several hours or longer. Serve as a garnish or condiment or add to a green salad.

Serves 3 to 4.

JALAPEÑOS RELLENOS
Stuffed jalapeños

> 4 *canned whole jalapeño chiles*
> 1 *cup Queso Blanco (see page 77) or queso fresco*

1. With a sharp knife slit each chile lengthwise along one side leaving the stem on. Rinse chiles; remove seeds.

2. Stuff the chiles with the cheese mixture and serve as a condiment.

Serves 2.

JALAPEÑO PEPPER JELLY

Recipients of a jar of this jelly will be so charmed they'll want to be on your gift list permanently. This jelly looks striking when made with red chiles and makes a delightful hors d'oeuvre when spread on crackers with cream cheese. It's also good as an accompaniment to barbecued meats or spread on corn bread.

> 3 *to 5 fresh jalapeño chiles, stemmed and seeded*
> 4 *medium-sized bell peppers*
> 1 *cup white vinegar*
> 5 *cups sugar*
> 1 *pouch (3 oz) liquid fruit pectin*

1. Grind jalapeño and bell peppers in a food mill or food processor, or mince with a knife.

2. Combine ground chiles and their juices, vinegar, and sugar in a 6-quart or larger pot; bring to a slow boil and boil 10 minutes.

3. Remove from heat and stir in pectin according to the directions on the package. Return to heat and bring to a boil; boil rapidly for 1 minute.

4. Remove from heat and skim off foam with a metal spoon.

5. Quickly ladle into hot, sterilized jars, leaving ½-inch headspace; seal.

Makes 4 cups.

Sopa de Melón Escribe—cantaloupe soup—(page 34) is a delicate yet flavorful soup ideal as a first course or for a summer lunch.

Soups & Dry Soups

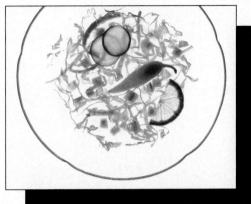

Mexican soups range from a light and delicate squash- or pumpkin-blossom soup to *pozole*, a hearty main-dish soup, to the rich and unusual *sopas secas* or dry soups. Chiles and other native ingredients add zest and variety to these soups, making them an unusual and welcome departure from standard soup fare. Instead of a plain rice or vermicelli side dish, Mexicans prefer the more elaborate and flavorful dry soups.

SOPAS—SOUPS

Soups play an important role in the cuisine of Mexico. The soup that begins the *comida mexicana* (the main meal of the day) is a *caldo* or light soup, often as simple as a clear broth with garnishes, but sometimes a more elaborate light and delicate cream soup laced with a dash of sherry. These cream soups are a wonderful example of the French influence found throughout Mexican cuisine.

The soup kitchen of Mexico also includes many hearty soups, called *sopas*. These main-course soups may contain two or more meats as well as vegetables and garnishes, the combination making a colorful, hearty, and delicious main course.

When in Mexico, a dinner without soup is considered only a snack.

Cooking Notes

Please note that the salt indicated in each recipe of this chapter is only a suggested amount. The amount of salt you add will vary depending on the seasoning of the broth and individual taste.

The use of cilantro in all recipes in this chapter is optional. Certainly it adds another dimension of flavor and is used extensively in the cuisine, so use it if available. There is no substitute. If cilantro is unavailable, simply omit it.

Some canned products will work well in the sopa and sopa seca recipes, such as canned chicken broth, canned whole tomatoes, and canned green chiles. These canned foods may be substituted when fresh ingredients are not available, and will be a convenient time saver when your schedule is busy.

SOPA DE FLOR DE CALABAZA
Squash or pumpkin blossom soup

Squash blossoms were used by the Aztecs and are still used today in recipes such as this delicate soup. Garnish the soup with some small blossoms for a finishing touch.

- 1 pound squash or pumpkin blossoms
- 2 tablespoons butter
  Half a small onion, finely chopped
- 4 cups chicken broth
  Sprig of epazote, if available
  Salt to taste

1. Wash blossoms, pat dry with a paper towel, and coarsely chop.

2. In a soup pot melt butter and gently sauté the blossoms and onion over medium heat. Add chicken broth and epazote. Simmer 20 minutes.

3. Remove the epazote, add salt to taste, and serve.

Serves 6.

Variation For cream soup, follow the above method, adding 1 cup half-and-half just before serving; allow to heat through.

CREMA DE AGUACATE
Cream of avocado soup

- 2 large, ripe avocados, cut in half
- 1 cup half-and-half
- 1 tablespoon fresh lime or lemon juice
- ¼ teaspoon salt
- 2 cups chicken broth
- ¼ cup dry sherry
  Thin lime slices, for garnish

1. Scoop the avocado from the peel and place it in a blender or food processor together with the half-and-half, lime juice, and salt. Blend to a smooth purée.

2. Heat chicken broth. Pour purée into warmed bowls or a tureen. Slowly stir in the hot broth, then the sherry.

3. Garnish each bowl with a thin slice of lime. This soup may be served warm or chilled. To reheat, use a double boiler.

Serves 6.

SOPA DE CHILE VERDE
Green chile soup

You can use a combination of bell peppers and mild, long green chiles to approximate the flavor of the poblano chile, favored in Mexico but not always found in the United States.

- 6 poblano chiles, roasted, peeled, and cleaned (if unavailable, use 2 bell peppers, seeded and chopped, and 4 mild, long green chiles, roasted, peeled, and cleaned)
- 1 small onion, chopped
- ½ cup whipping cream
- 2 tablespoons butter
- 2 tablespoons flour
- 4 cups chicken broth
  Salt to taste
  Sour cream, for garnish

1. Place chiles in a blender or food processor together with the onion and cream. Blend until smooth; use small amounts of the broth, if necessary, to blend.

2. Melt butter over medium heat in a medium saucepan. Gradually add flour, stirring constantly. Gradually add the chile purée, stirring constantly. Slowly stir in the broth. Add salt to taste.

3. Stir the soup over medium heat until thickened and smooth. Serve topped with a dab of sour cream.

Serves 6.

SOPA DE FIDEO
Vermicelli soup

This full-flavored soup contains one of the few types of pasta used in Mexico. It can be served as a side dish or as a first course.

- 1 package (8 oz) coiled vermicelli, broken
- ¼ cup oil
  Half an onion, chopped
- 1 clove garlic, minced
- 1 mild, long green chile, seeded and chopped (not roasted)
- 2 tomatoes, chopped
- 8 cups chicken broth
  Salt to taste
- ¼ pound jack cheese, cut in small cubes

1. A convenient way to crumble the vermicelli is to roll a rolling pin over the unopened package. Heat oil over medium heat in a soup pot. Sauté the vermicelli in the oil until golden, stirring constantly (it scorches easily).

2. Push the vermicelli to one side, add the onion, garlic, and chile, and cook until onion is soft. Add tomato and cook until soft.

3. Add broth and season to taste. Simmer until the vermicelli is tender, about 15 minutes.

4. To serve, place a few cubes of cheese in each bowl and ladle the hot soup over the cheese.

Serves 6 to 8.

HEARTY POZOLE DINNER

Pozole

Tortillas

Mexican Beer

Capirotada
(see page 122)

Café de Olla
(see page 123)

For adventuresome types who enjoy discovering why certain dishes become mainstays of cuisines, Pozole is the Mexican answer. Pozole, a pork and hominy soup, served with garnishes of lime wedges, crisp pork rinds, avocado pieces, onions, or radishes, may strike people as unusual fare at first, but once they savor its flavors they will always return for more.

POZOLE
Pork and hominy soup

There are many versions of *pozole*. Most start with corn, the type called *cacahuazincle*, which is made into hominy. Some versions add beans or substitute garbanzos for the hominy. This deluxe version, Pozole de Lujo, adds pork loin and chicken. This recipe originated in Guadalajara. It's perfect for a cold day. You may omit the pig's feet without losing significant flavor but they do make the dish authentic.

- 2 pig's feet, split
- 1 pound fresh pork loin or hocks, trimmed and cut into chunks
- 3 large cloves garlic, minced
- 1 large onion, coarsely chopped
- 1 bay leaf
- 4 quarts water
- 1 3 pound chicken, cut up
- 2 cans (29 oz each) hominy, drained
- 2 teaspoons salt
  Garnishes: Shredded cabbage, chopped onions, chopped radishes, lime wedges, salsa or jalapeño slices, crumbled dried oregano

1. Place the pig's feet, pork, garlic, onion, bay leaf, and enough water to cover in a large soup pot. Bring to a boil, then simmer covered for 1 hour.

2. Add chicken and continue to cook until almost tender, about 40 minutes.

3. Add hominy and salt. Cook for 30 minutes more.

4. Prepare garnishes and place in small bowls. Serve the soup with the garnishes available separately.

Serves 12.

Served with hot tortillas or bolillos, Mexican chicken soup—chicken, carrots, zucchini, chayote, and corn in a clear broth—makes a great meal.

MEXICAN SOUP FARE

Guacamole (see page 40)

Sopaipillas (see page 123)

Sopa de Pollo or Sopa de Pollo y Aguacate

Mexican Beer

Empanadas de Piña (see page 121)

For a hearty yet elegant dinner with a Mexican theme, try one of these luscious chicken soups accompanied by guacamole and the deep-fried puffs of dough called sopaipillas. The soups are easy to make and will surely be enjoyed by everyone. You can make both the sopaipillas and the soup ahead and reheat them when needed. The pineapple empanadas or turnovers are a refreshing end to the meal.

SOPA DE POLLO
Chicken soup

Chicken soup is a classic in any cuisine. This is Mexico's version. The vegetables are cut for eye appeal as well as for eating convenience. They are then added to the soup pot according to their cooking time.

- 1 onion, chopped
- 2 cloves garlic, minced
- 1 tablespoon oil
- 1 3½-pound chicken, cut up
- 1 teaspoon salt
- 2 chayotes, cut in half lengthwise
- 6 carrots, cut in half lengthwise, then into thirds
- 3 ears corn, cut into thirds
- 3 zucchini, cut into chunks
  Lime wedges, oregano, and salsa, for garnish

1. In a large soup pot, sauté onion and garlic in oil over medium heat. Add chicken and cover with water. Add salt. Bring almost to a boil, reduce heat, cover, and simmer the chicken until tender, about 30 to 40 minutes.

2. In another pot, cover chayotes with water and bring to a boil. Reduce heat, cover, and cook until almost tender, about 15 minutes. Drain the chayotes and allow to cool. Peel and cut into large chunks, then set aside.

3. Remove the chicken; skin and bone, if desired, and cut the chicken meat into serving-sized pieces.

4. Add carrots and corn to the soup pot and simmer 10 minutes. Add the zucchini and cook an additional 10 minutes. Add chayote and chicken pieces and continue cooking until the zucchini is tender and the chayote and chicken are heated through. Check the seasoning; add salt to taste.

5. In each bowl place a piece of chicken and some of each of the vegetables, then ladle the broth over all. Serve lime wedges, oregano, and your favorite salsa in separate bowls.

Serves 6.

SOPA DE POLLO Y AGUACATE
Chicken and avocado soup

This version of chicken soup includes avocados and green beans.

- 1 3- to 3½-pound chicken, cut up
- 1 stalk celery, thinly sliced
- 2 medium carrots, chopped
- 2 medium onions, slivered
- 1 large clove garlic, minced or pressed
- 1 teaspoon each salt and whole cumin seed, crushed
- ½ teaspoon dried oregano
- 2 small, hot, dried red chiles, crushed
- 6 cups water
- 2 cups cut green beans (fresh or frozen)
- 2 medium tomatoes, seeded and chopped
- ¼ cup chopped cilantro
- 1 large avocado, peeled, seeded, and thinly sliced
  Lime wedges, for garnish

1. In a 5- to 6-quart kettle or Dutch oven, combine chicken, celery, carrots, onions, garlic, salt, cumin seed, oregano, chiles, and water. Bring slowly to a boil; then cover, reduce heat, and simmer until chicken is very tender and broth is flavorful (2 to 2½ hours).

2. Remove chicken pieces; discard bones and skin, and separate meat into chunks. (You can do this much ahead; wrap and refrigerate meat, and cover and refrigerate soup.) Skim and discard fat from surface of broth.

3. Bring soup to a boil, add green beans, and cook, uncovered, for 5 minutes. Add chicken, reduce heat, and cook until it is heated through (3 to 5 minutes). Taste, and add salt if needed. Mix in tomatoes, cilantro, and avocado slices.

4. Serve with lime wedges to squeeze into each bowl of soup to taste.

Serves 6.

SOPA DE ALBÓNDIGAS
Meatball soup

Albóndigas, translated, simply means meatballs, but in Mexico it most often refers to this soup in which meatballs are the main ingredient. The distinctive flavor of yerba buena (mint) gives an added dimension to the flavor of the soup. The soup is not authentic without it. Like many soups, albóndigas acquires its fullest flavor if prepared a day in advance, especially if water is used instead of stock.

Albóndigas
Meatballs

1 pound lean ground beef
Half an onion, minced
2 tablespoons bread crumbs
1 tablespoon fresh mint, minced, or 1 teaspoon dried mint, crushed
1 egg, slightly beaten
½ teaspoon salt
Pinch ground cumin (optional)
2 tablespoons raw rice

Caldo
Broth

1 can (16 oz) whole tomatoes
Half an onion, chopped
2 cloves garlic, minced
1 tablespoon oil
6 cups beef or chicken stock (or water)
2 carrots, sliced
2 zucchini, sliced
½ teaspoon salt, or to taste
Salsa and sour cream, for garnish

1. Place all the ingredients for the albóndigas in a bowl and mix together thoroughly. Form small meatballs. Moisten your hands frequently with cold water to prevent the meat from sticking.

2. Drain the juice from the tomatoes and reserve. Coarsely chop the tomatoes. Set aside.

3. In a soup pot, sauté onion and garlic in oil until soft. Add the stock or water and bring to a boil. Slowly add the meatballs and bring to a second boil; skim if necessary. Reduce heat, add the tomatoes and their juice. Cover and simmer 20 minutes. If water is used in place of stock, the meatballs make an adequate stock of their own.

4. Add carrots and zucchini. Check the seasoning and add salt if necessary. Cover and continue cooking for 30 minutes.

5. Serve the salsa and sour cream separately.

Serves 6 to 8.

SOPA DE LIMA
Lime soup

Strictly translated we would have to call this lemon soup in English. In the Yucatán, where this recipe originates, it is made from Yucatecan limas agrias, which translates as sour lemons. Some Mexican recipes suggest using one lime and one lemon to approximate the taste; another suggests adding grapefruit rind. It's great using just limes, and the soup has a wonderfully refreshing flavor.

6 to 8 corn tortillas, cut into wedges
Salt
Oil ¼ inch deep, for frying
4 chicken breasts, boned
8 cups chicken broth
1 onion, quartered
3 cloves garlic, coarsely chopped
6 peppercorns
½ teaspoon thyme
1 tablespoon oil
Half an onion, chopped
2 large, mild green chiles, seeded and chopped (not roasted)
2 tomatoes, peeled and chopped
1 teaspoon salt
6 limes
⅓ cup cilantro
2 avocados

1. Fresh tortillas will not work well for this recipe. Cut tortillas into wedges. Spread a single layer on a baking sheet and allow to air-dry or dry in a 200° F oven for approximately 20 minutes.

2. Lightly salt the tortilla wedges and fry in hot oil (400° F) until hardened but not brown and crispy. Drain on paper towels and set aside.

3. In a large soup pot, place chicken breasts, broth, the quartered onion, garlic, peppercorns, and thyme. Bring almost to a boil, reduce heat, cover, and simmer 20 minutes. Allow chicken to cool in the broth.

4. Remove the chicken from the pot. Discard the skin and bones and shred the meat. Strain the broth into a separate container.

5. In the soup pot, heat the 1 tablespoon oil and sauté the chopped onion and chiles over medium heat. Cook until the onion is soft. Add the tomatoes and cook until soft.

6. Return the broth to the soup pot, add the 1 teaspoon salt, and bring to a boil. Reduce heat and add the juice of 3 or 4 of the limes, plus a squeezed lime half. Simmer 20 minutes.

7. Remove the lime half, add the shredded chicken, and simmer 10 minutes. Stir in the cilantro. Reheat the tortilla wedges in a 350° F oven for 10 minutes.

8. Cut the avocados in half, seed, peel, and cut into slices. Cut the remaining limes into wedges.

9. Ladle the soup into serving bowls and drop hot tortilla wedges into each bowl. Serve the avocado slices and lime wedges separately.

Serves 8.

Sopa de Lima, or lime soup, features chicken in a broth accented with the flavors of lime, cilantro, and thyme. The avocado adds an elegant touch.

MENUDO
Tripe soup

To hear Mexicans talk of the beneficial effects of menudo, one would expect to find it included in the pharmacopoeia, along with other medicines and remedies, instead of in a cookbook. It has the reputation for fighting the effects of the *cruda*, or hangover, and is therefore traditionally served on New Year's Day.

    1 calf's foot, cut into pieces
    3 pounds tripe, washed,
        trimmed of fat, and cut
        into 1-inch squares
    4 quarts water
    2 teaspoons salt
    3 ancho chiles (see Note)
    1 California chile (see Note)
    1 large onion, chopped
    3 cloves garlic, crushed
    1 teaspoon freshly ground
        black pepper
    2 cans (29 oz each)
        hominy, drained, or 5 cups
        cooked hominy
    ½ cup fresh cilantro
        Garnishes: lime wedges,
        chopped onion, fresh
        mint, dried oregano, crushed
        japonés chile, salsa, or sliced
        jalapeños

1. Place the calf's foot, tripe, water, and salt in a large soup pot. Bring to a boil, reduce heat, and simmer, uncovered, for 2½ hours, skimming the top occasionally.

2. Remove the stems and seeds from the chiles, crumble them into a blender, and blend until finely ground.

3. Remove the calf's foot from the pot. Remove any meat remaining on the bones and discard the bones. Coarsely chop the meat and add it back to the soup. Add the onion, garlic, pepper, and ground chiles and continue to cook, uncovered, for another 2½ hours.

4. Add the hominy and bring the soup to a boil; reduce heat and simmer 1 to 2 hours more. The soup will be finished in 1 hour, but an additional hour of cooking will improve the flavor. Stir in the cilantro the last half hour of cooking.

5. Serve the soup with the garnishes available separately.

Serves 8.

<u>Note</u> 2 to 3 tablespoons mild, ground red chile without spices may be substituted for the ancho and California chiles.

FRIJOLES CHARROS
Cowboy bean soup

    4 slices bacon, each strip
        cut into eighths
    1 large onion, coarsely chopped
    2 cloves garlic, minced
    2 cups dry pinto beans, washed
    8 cups water
    3 mild, long green chiles, roast-
        ed, peeled, cleaned, and cut
        into strips (¼ inch wide and
        2 inches long)
    3 tomatoes, peeled and cut
        into chunks
    1½ teaspoons salt

1. In a large soup pot, cook bacon until crisp. Add onion and garlic and cook until onion is soft.

2. Add uncooked beans and water. Bring to a boil, reduce heat, cover, and simmer just until the skin begins to split on the beans, about 2¼ hours.

3. Add chiles, tomato, and salt. Continue cooking until the beans are very tender and fully cooked, about 30 minutes. Check the seasoning and serve.

Serves 10.

SOPA DE PAPAS Y CHILE VERDE
Potato and green chile soup

    Half an onion, chopped
    1 clove garlic, minced
    3 poblano chiles, roasted,
        peeled, cleaned, and chopped
        (if unavailable, use 3 mild,
        long green chiles)
    1 tablespoon oil
    1 tomato, chopped
    4 cups chicken broth, heated
    3 medium potatoes, cubed
    ¼ teaspoon oregano
    ¼ pound jack cheese, grated
        Salt to taste

1. In a soup pot sauté over medium heat onion, garlic, and chile in the oil until onion is soft. Add tomato and cook until soft.

2. Add heated broth and potatoes. When potatoes are tender, add oregano and cheese. Add salt to taste. When cheese has melted, stir and serve.

Serves 4 to 6.

SOPA DE MELÓN ESCRIBE
Cantaloupe soup

Not only unusual, this soup is a delicate surprise. Perfect for summer, it can be served for any light meal from brunch to dinner.

    ½ cup half-and-half
    1 cup cooked, peeled, and
        diced potato
    3 cups peeled, diced cantaloupe
    ¼ cup dry sherry
        Pinch salt
        Freshly ground nutmeg,
        for garnish

1. Place half-and-half, potato, and cantaloupe in a blender or food processor. Blend to a smooth purée.

2. Stir in sherry. Add salt.

3. Serve chilled, sprinkled with freshly ground nutmeg.

Serves 6.

SOPA DE TORTILLA
Tortilla soup

This Mexican version of tomato soup can be used as a first-course soup or as the main course for a light meal. Simple and colorful, it is especially striking to serve on a buffet table. Serve the fried tortilla strips in a basket, the broth in a tureen, and the cheese in a colorful pottery bowl, and allow your guests to assemble their own soup.

    6 to 8 corn tortillas, cut into
       ¼-inch strips
       Oil ¼ inch deep, for frying
    1 tablespoon oil
       Half an onion, chopped
    2 cloves garlic, minced
       or crushed
    1 can (28 oz) solid-pack
       tomatoes, puréed
    4 cups chicken broth
    ⅓ cup fresh cilantro,
       slightly chopped
       Salt to taste
    ⅓ pound mild Cheddar,
       Colby, or jack cheese, grated

1. Spread a single layer of tortilla strips on a baking sheet and allow to air-dry or dry in a 200° F oven for approximately 20 minutes.

2. Fry tortilla strips in hot oil (400° F) until hardened but not brown or crispy. Drain on paper towels and set aside.

3. In a soup pot heat the 1 tablespoon oil; add onion and garlic. Cook until onion is soft. Add puréed tomatoes and chicken stock and bring to a boil. Reduce heat and simmer for 10 minutes. Add cilantro and salt to taste.

4. *To serve:* In the bottom of each serving bowl, place a handful of the prepared tortilla strips. Ladle the soup over the strips and top with grated cheese.

Serves 8.

Variation Cook 1 can (4 oz) diced green chiles with the onion and garlic. Add ½ cup shredded chicken for the last 5 minutes of simmering.

SOPAS SECAS— DRY SOUPS

The *sopa seca*, the dry soup, the soupless soup! Sopa seca is made of rice cooked in a broth with onions, garlic, and tomatoes. As the rice cooks, the broth cooks away and is completely absorbed into the rice. The sopa seca we see most often is a rice dish that is invariably served with the meal in Mexican restaurants. Although the classic sopa seca is made with *arroz* (rice), it can also be made with any of the few pastas used in Mexico, and some may even be made with pieces of corn tortilla.

While on the subject of rice in the Mexican cuisine, one point needs special clarification. While rice was introduced to Mexico from Spain, there is no dish called Spanish Rice in the Mexican cuisine. This main dish, served in many homes in the United States, has no counterpart in Mexico, and should not be thought of as a Mexican recipe.

Cooking Notes

The secret of perfect texture in the sopa seca recipes is in paying close attention during two of the cooking steps. The first step is cooking the rice in the oil. The oil must be heated so that the rice begins to cook immediately when placed in the skillet. Test the oil by dropping one grain of rice into the oil. When it begins to cook and puff slightly, the oil is ready. Sauté the rice, stirring constantly as the grains puff and brown, until all are evenly cooked.

The second important step is to allow all of the broth to be absorbed during the final cooking process. Each grain should be separate. To achieve this texture, it is important to use only long-grain rice, not a converted or quick rice. Refer also to the cooking notes at the beginning of this chapter under "Sopas— Soups"; they apply as well to the sopas secas.

If you use canned broth, additional salt will not be necessary.

ARROZ A LA MEXICANA
Mexican-style rice

This is the most classic and traditional sopa seca. The flavors of the vegetables and chicken broth make this rice especially delicious.

    3   tablespoons oil
    1   cup long-grain rice
        Half an onion, chopped
    1   clove garlic, minced
    1   tomato, chopped
    2½ cups chicken broth
    ¼   cup fresh or frozen peas
        (optional)
        Salt to taste

1. Heat the oil in a large skillet. Add rice and cook over medium heat stirring constantly, until puffed and golden.

2. Push the rice to one side, add onion and garlic, and cook until the onion is soft. Add tomato and cook briefly until soft. Stir to mix rice into onion/tomato mixture.

3. Add chicken broth, bring to a boil. Reduce heat, cover, and simmer for 20 minutes. Add the peas (if used) by placing them on top of the rice; do not stir. Cover and continue cooking until all liquid has been absorbed (10 to 15 minutes longer). Add salt to taste. Toss lightly with a fork before serving.

Serves 4 to 6.

Step·by·step

HOW TO MAKE A SOPA SECA

Here we show you how to make Fideo, a dry soup made with vermicelli. Sopas secas made from rice follow a similar procedure.

1. *Take a rolling pin and roll over the unopened package of vermicelli until it is crumbled. Heat oil in a large skillet over a burner. Add the crumbled vermicelli and stir with a wooden spoon. Because the vermicelli scorches easily (more easily than rice), stir it constantly while browning in oil.*

2. *Push the browned vermicelli to one side of the skillet and cook the vegetables, in this case onions, garlic, green pepper and tomatoes, until the onion is soft and the vegetables are cooked.*

3. *After the vegetables have cooked, mix them with the vermicelli. Add boiling stock, cover, and steam until liquid is absorbed.*

FIDEO
Vermicelli

Although not commonly served in restaurants, this sopa seca is a favorite in Mexican homes.

- 1 package (8 oz) coiled vermicelli, broken
- ¼ cup oil
- ½ onion, chopped
- 1 clove garlic, minced
- 1 mild, long green chile, seeded and chopped (optional)
- 1 tomato, chopped
- 2½ cups chicken broth
  Salt to taste
  Sour cream and fresh cilantro, for garnish

1. To crumble the vermicelli, roll a rolling pin over the unopened package. Heat oil over medium heat in a large skillet. Sauté the vermicelli in the oil until golden, stirring constantly. Vermicelli is more delicate than rice and scorches easily.

2. Push the vermicelli to one side, add onion, garlic, and chile, and cook until the onion is soft. Add tomato and stir to mix vermicelli with chile/tomato mixture.

3. Add broth and bring to a boil. Reduce heat, cover, and simmer until the liquid has been absorbed (15 to 20 minutes). Check seasoning and add salt if necessary.

4. Serve garnished with a dab of sour cream and a few fresh cilantro leaves.

Serves 4 to 6.

Variation Alphabet pasta is another pasta typically used in Mexico and it may be substituted for the vermicelli. Increase the broth by ½ cup. For a delicious liquid soup, add 4 to 5 cups broth.

ARROZ BLANCO
White rice

- 3 tablespoons oil
- 1 clove garlic
- 1 cup long-grain rice
  Half an onion, diced
- 2½ cups chicken broth
  Salt to taste

1. Heat the oil with the garlic in a skillet. Cook until garlic is golden brown; remove and discard garlic.

2. Add rice and cook, stirring constantly, until puffed (do not cook the rice until golden). Push the rice to one side, add the onion, and sauté until soft. Stir to mix the onion and rice together.

3. Add chicken broth and bring to a boil. Reduce heat, cover, and simmer until all liquid has been absorbed (about 30 to 35 minutes). Check the seasoning and add salt to taste if necessary. Toss lightly with a fork before serving.

Serves 4 to 6.

ARROZ VERDE
Green rice

The piquant flavors of chiles and cilantro make this rice dish a favorite.

- 2 poblano chiles, roasted, peeled, cleaned, and seeded (if unavailable, use 1 large, mild green chile, roasted, peeled, cleaned, and seeded, and *half a bell pepper, seeded and chopped*)
- ½ cup fresh cilantro
- 2½ cups chicken broth
- 3 tablespoons oil
- 1 cup long-grain rice
  Half an onion, chopped
- 1 clove garlic, minced
  Salt to taste

1. Place chiles and cilantro in a blender or food processor with ½ cup of the chicken broth. Blend to a smooth purée.

2. Heat the oil in a skillet. Add rice and cook, stirring constantly, until puffed and golden.

3. Push the rice to one side, add onion and garlic, and cook.

4. Add remaining chicken broth and bring to a boil. Reduce heat, cover, and simmer until all liquid has been absorbed (about 30 to 35 minutes). Check seasoning and add salt if necessary. Toss lightly with a fork before serving.

Serves 4 to 6.

ARROZ GUALDO
Yellow rice

This rice, colored and delicately flavored with achiote, is typical of Yucatán. Achiote, the small, brick-red seed of the annatto tree, imparts a bright yellow color to the rice and gives it a flavor that is especially tasty with fish dishes.

> 1½ teaspoons achiote (annatto seed)
> 3 tablespoons oil
> 1 cup long-grain rice
>   Half a small onion, chopped
> 1 clove garlic, minced
> 2 cups chicken stock or water
> 1 teaspoon salt

1. In a medium saucepan over low heat, fry achiote in oil. Remove the seeds from the oil when they are dark brown, and discard seeds. The oil will be dark orange in color.

2. Add the washed, drained rice to the oil and sauté for about 5 minutes. Add the onion and garlic and cook until onion is soft.

3. In a separate pan bring stock to a boil. Add boiling stock to rice along with salt. Bring mixture to a boil, lower the flame, cover, and cook until liquid is absorbed (20 to 25 minutes).

Serves 4 to 6.

ARROZ DE MEXICO
Mexican rice

This is a simplified version of the traditional Arroz a la Mexicana.

> 3 tablespoons oil
> 1 cup long-grain rice
> ½ onion, chopped
> 1 clove garlic, minced
> 1 cup mild green chile salsa
> 2 cups chicken broth
>   Fresh cilantro, for garnish (optional)

1. Heat the oil in a skillet. Add rice and cook over medium heat stirring constantly, until puffed and golden.

2. Push the rice to one side, add onion and garlic, and cook until onion is soft. Add salsa and cook briefly, stirring to mix rice with onion/salsa mixture.

3. Add chicken broth and bring to a boil. Reduce heat, cover, and simmer until all liquid has been absorbed (about 30 to 35 minutes). Garnish with cilantro, if desired.

Serves 4 to 6.

Arroz Gualdo, Mexican yellow rice, surrounded by sliced tomatoes makes a stunning, flavorful rice dish. The bright yellow color is imparted by achiote (annatto seed).

The natural beauty and flavor of fresh vegetables is difficult to surpass. Squash, peas, avocado, jicama, lettuce, chayote, and more are featured here.

Salads & Vegetables

Although we don't often think of salads or vegetable dishes when we plan a Mexican meal, they are incorporated into almost every meal. Mexico offers some unusual native vegetables—such as chayotes, nopales, jicama, and tomatillos—that are increasingly available in our markets. All of these will add interest to an otherwise ordinary salad or vegetable dish. Here you will discover the tastes and textures of Mexican vegetables and how they can best be used in various dishes.

SALADS

Salads served in Mexico range from simple garden green salads to cold marinated vegetable salads to fruit salads, one of which is featured traditionally in the Christmas Eve feast (see Ensalada de Noche Buena, page 43). You will find that some of these salads combine unusual ingredients, others use unfamiliar vegetables, and all provide interesting new ideas for meal planning.

CHAYOTE

The pale green chayote is a member of the squash family, native to Mexico. It has been grown in North Africa and exported to Europe for many years as a gourmet vegetable prized for its subtle texture and mild, delicate flavor. It is becoming increasingly available in markets throughout the United States.

Chayotes should be cut in half or quartered before cooking (the seed is tender and also edible when cooked). The chayotes are then peeled and ready to use as an ingredient. Do not try to peel the chayote before cooking, as the vegetable gives off a sticky substance when peeled raw that irritates the hands.

ENSALADA DE CHAYOTE
Chayote salad

3 chayotes
*1 small white onion, thinly
   sliced, separated into rings*
*2 tomatoes, cut into chunky
   bite-sized pieces*
*1 can (2¼ oz) sliced ripe
   olives, drained*
2 tablespoons chopped cilantro
*⅓ cup Oil and Vinegar Dressing
   (see page 44)
   Half a head green leaf
   lettuce, shredded*

1. Halve chayotes but do not peel; place in a steamer or cover with water in a saucepan; bring to a boil, reduce heat, cover, and cook until fork-tender (approximately 15 minutes). Allow to cool; peel and cut into chunky, bite-sized pieces.

2. In a bowl combine chayotes, onion, tomatoes, olives, and cilantro. Toss with Oil and Vinegar Dressing and chill. Arrange on a bed of shredded lettuce just before serving.

Serves 6.

GUACAMOLE
**Avocado salad or dip—
traditional version**

The avocado is used extensively in Mexico. Often just sliced and served as a garnish, it provides one of the important texture contrasts so typical of the cuisine. Certainly its most well known and popular use is in guacamole.

Guacamole is a versatile dish. In Mexico it is most often served on lettuce as a salad or side dish, but it is used also as a garnish for tacos, burritos, tostadas, or flautas and, of course, as a dip accompanied by Totopos (fried tortilla wedges; see page 62) or assorted raw vegetables.

2 large avocados
*2 teaspoons fresh lime or
   lemon juice*
¼ cup sour cream (optional)
1 small clove garlic, crushed
1 small tomato, diced
*1 canned jalapeño, seeded and
   finely chopped (optional)*
*¼ cup onion, finely minced
   Few sprigs cilantro,
   coarsely chopped*

1. Halve the avocados; remove pit, scoop out pulp, and mash with a fork.

2. Add lime juice, sour cream (if used), garlic, tomato, jalapeño (if used), and cilantro, mixing after each addition.

Makes approximately 2½ cups.

GUACAMOLE
**Avocado dip—
simplified version**

2 large avocados
⅓ cup salsa (see pages 20-23)

1. Halve the avocados; remove seed, scoop out pulp, and mash with a fork.

2. Combine avocado and salsa and mix well.

Makes approximately 2 cups.

GUACAMOLE CON TOMATILLOS
**Avocado dip with Mexican
green tomatoes**

The unusual lemony flavor of tomatillos and the cilantro make this recipe very distinctive.

*4 or 5 fresh or canned
   tomatillos*
*3 canned green chiles, seeded
   (or 1 serrano or jalapeño
   chile, if hotter sauce is desired)*
2 large avocados
*1 tablespoon minced onion
   Salt and pepper*
*¼ cup cilantro leaves, minced,
   for garnish*

1. If using fresh tomatillos, discard husks and wash tomatillos. Boil in a small amount of water until just tender, about 5 minutes. Drain.

2. If using one of the hotter fresh chiles, discard stem and seeds. Combine tomatillos and chiles in a blender and blend until smooth.

3. Halve the avocados and remove seed. Scoop out pulp and mash with a fork. Stir in tomatillo mixture and onions. Add salt and pepper to taste. Sprinkle cilantro over top.

Makes 2½ cups.

Guacamole served with freshly made tortilla chips and crisp vegetables makes a festive and colorful hors d'oeuvre that is perfect for a summer barbecue.

The pads of different varieties of prickly pear plants vary considerably in the number and sharpness of their spines. Those with very sharp spines must be handled with tongs, using great care. You may be lucky enough to find fresh nopales that have had the spines removed or a thornless variety, *Opuntia basilaris.*

To Prepare Fresh Nopales

1. Select young, firm nopales (cactus pads), trim the spines, and dice into ½-inch pieces.

2. Place the nopales in boiling, salted water to cover; reduce heat and simmer until tender (approximately 10 to 15 minutes).

3. Rinse and drain several times until no longer slippery. The cactus is now ready to use.

Note To prepare canned nopales, rinse and drain several times until no longer slippery.

ENSALADA DE NOPALITOS
Cactus salad

> 2 to 3 cups freshly prepared nopales (see page 12) or 1 jar (16 to 20 oz) nopales
> 1 small red onion, thinly sliced and separated into rings
> 3 tomatoes, chopped
> 1 can (4¼ oz) sliced ripe olives, drained
> 2 tablespoons cilantro leaves, chopped
> ⅓ cup Oil and Vinegar Dressing (see page 44)

Mix together nopales, onion, tomatoes, olives, and cilantro. Toss with Oil and Vinegar Dressing, and serve.

Serves 6.

Nopales, red onions, tomatoes, ripe olives, cilantro, and more combine to make a stunning salad with a special flavor. Your adventuresome friends will love the idea of eating the pad of a prickly pear cactus. But don't worry—they taste like green beans.

NOPALES
Cactus sections

Nopales are the "leaves" or pads of the prickly pear cactus. In the United States fresh nopales are common in markets in the Southwest and can be found in some supermarkets in other parts of the country. Nopales may also be purchased ready to use in jars as *nopalitos*, meaning small cactus pieces (diced cactus). Prepared nopales are somewhat like green beans in taste and texture, with a slight tartness that is quite special.

JICAMA

Jicama is a brown-skinned root common throughout Mexico. It looks like a sugar beet but when peeled it is crisp and pure white and similar to an apple in texture. Although technically a vegetable, jicama is the mainstay of the fruit vendor's cart and is used as a fruit in Mexico, often in combination with other fruits in salads. It is the major ingredient in Ensalada de Noche Buena, a salad traditionally served on Christmas Eve.

Jicama is a wonderful vegetable to use with dips. It stays fresh and crisp, it does not turn brown after being cut, and its pure white color contrasts nicely with other "dip" vegetables.

When shopping for jicama, look for one with a smooth firmness and uniformity to the skin to ensure a fresh, crisp texture.

ENSALADA DE NOCHE BUENA
Christmas Eve salad

- 1 large jicama, peeled and cut into bite-sized pieces
- 2 oranges, peeled, sliced, and quartered
- 3 slices fresh pineapple, peeled and cut into bite-sized pieces
- 2 bananas, sliced
- 8 ounces diced canned beets (optional)
  Half a head iceberg lettuce, shredded
- ½ cup unsalted peanuts
  Seeds from 1 pomegranate

1. In a bowl mix together the jicama, oranges, and pineapple and chill for at least 1 hour.

2. Just before serving add bananas and beets (if used).

3. Line a salad bowl or platter with lettuce and arrange fruit on the lettuce. Garnish with peanuts and pomegranate seeds.

Serves 6 to 8.

ENSALADA DE JICAMA Y NARANJAS
Jicama and orange salad

- 1 small jicama, peeled and diced
  Half a cucumber, scored with a fork and thinly sliced
- 3 oranges, peeled, sliced, and quartered
- ⅓ cup Oil and Vinegar Dressing (see page 44)
  Green leaf lettuce

1. Mix together jicama, cucumber, and oranges. Toss with dressing and chill until ready to serve.

2. Just before serving, line a platter or individual plates with lettuce leaves and arrange salad on the lettuce.

Serves 4 to 6.

Jicama, cucumber, and orange, tossed with Oil and Vinegar Dressing, combine to create an unusual taste treat. This salad has a pleasing, tangy sweetness.

JICAMA CON CHILE Y LIMON
Jicama with chile and lime

Jicama con chile y limon is commonly sold from little carts on the streets of Mexico.

1 small jicama, peeled and cut into bite-sized wedges
Salt
Ground red chile, mild or hot, according to taste
2 limes, cut into wedges

1. Place the jicama wedges on toothpicks and arrange on a platter. Sprinkle with salt and ground chile.

2. Serve with the lime wedges; each person squeezes a little lime juice over the jicama before eating.

Serves 6 to 8.

ENSALADA DE PIMIENTOS
Pimiento salad

This dish is most often prepared with red pimientos, but it is even more colorful made with red and green bell peppers.

1 pound red pimientos (or combination of red and green bell peppers)
1 small onion, sliced into thin rounds
1 tomato, cut in half-slices
3 tablespoons olive oil
2 tablespoons vinegar
Salt and pepper to taste

1. Roast the pimientos or bell peppers over an open flame or in a broiler until their skin is blackened (see page 17). As they are done, put them in a plastic bag to steam. After a few minutes they should peel easily.

2. Cut the stems from the peeled peppers and remove the seeds. Cut into narrow strips and arrange on a serving platter. Top with onion rounds. Surround with the half-slices of tomato.

3. Mix together the oil, vinegar, and salt and pepper; pour mixture over the peppers.

Serves 4.

ENSALADA DE CALABACITAS
Zucchini salad

2 pounds small zucchini
Half a white or red onion, thinly sliced and separated into rings
3 large, mild green chiles, roasted, peeled, seeded, and cut into thin strips, or 1 can (4 oz) diced whole green chiles, drained
1 can (2¼ oz) sliced ripe olives, drained
⅓ cup Oil and Vinegar Dressing (at right)
1 avocado, peeled, seeded, and cubed
¼ cup crumbled queso fresco (Mexican cheese) or feta cheese

1. Cut zucchini crosswise into ½-inch slices. Place in a steamer or cover with water in a saucepan; bring to a boil, reduce heat, cover, and cook until barely tender (approximately 5 to 8 minutes); do not overcook. Drain and rinse in cold water.

2. Combine zucchini, onion, chiles, and olives; mix with Oil and Vinegar Dressing. Chill at least 2 hours.

3. Just before serving stir in the avocado and top with the crumbled cheese.

Serves 6.

PICO DE GALLO
Rooster's beak

This favorite appetizer or snack is called rooster's beak because it is commonly eaten with finger and thumb, suggesting the pecking of a rooster. It is also served as a first course.

1 jicama, peeled and cut into bite-sized wedges
3 oranges, peeled and cut into bite-sized wedges
Salt
Ground unseasoned red chile, mild or hot, according to taste

1. Arrange the jicama and orange wedges on a platter or individual plates.

2. Pass shakers of salt and ground chile, allowing each person to season to taste.

Serves 6.

EJOTES Y PAPAS
Green beans and potatoes

1 pound small green beans, ends removed
6 small red potatoes, quartered
½ cup Oil and Vinegar Dressing (below)
2 tablespoons cilantro leaves, chopped
1 tablespoon capers
Green leaf lettuce

1. Place potatoes in a steamer and arrange green beans on top. Cover tightly and steam until barely tender (approximately 15 minutes). Do not overcook. Place vegetables in a bowl and mix with the dressing. Chill 3 hours.

2. Just before serving mix in the cilantro and capers. Line a platter or individual plates with lettuce leaves and arrange vegetables on the lettuce.

Serves 6.

OIL AND VINEGAR DRESSING

1 or 2 cloves garlic, crushed
¼ cup white wine vinegar
½ teaspoon salt
¼ teaspoon pepper
1 teaspoon dry or Dijon mustard
¾ cup oil (half olive oil and half salad oil)

1. Combine garlic, vinegar, salt, and pepper in a jar. Shake until the salt dissolves.

2. Add mustard and oil and shake until thoroughly blended.

Makes approximately 1 cup.

Fresh green beans, baby red potatoes, piquant capers, and an Oil and Vinegar Dressing combine to make a striking salad that's perfect for lunch.

Sweet corn on the cob, irresistible to begin with, is even more delicious when it is dipped in cream and rolled in sharp, tangy queso anejo or Parmesan cheese.

VERDURAS—COOKED VEGETABLES

Although cooked vegetables are an important part of the Mexican meal, unadorned vegetables have very little place on the Mexican table. Often fresh vegetables such as chiles, zucchini, green peas, and corn are dipped in a batter and fried much like fritters. They may also be cooked in the puddinglike *budín*—a batter made with flour, cheese, and eggs—or creamed, as in Elote con Crema (at right) or Chile con Queso (see page 50).

Many vegetables are typically combined with other vegetables and seasoned to make delicious and satisfying side dishes. If a vegetable is simply boiled or steamed, it is sure to be topped with a special sauce such as Salsa de Jalapeños Rojos (red jalapeño sauce, page 22).

ELOTE
Corn on the cob with cheese

This simple corn recipe, as prepared in Mexico, adds a new interest to an American favorite, corn on the cob. In Mexico the traditional cheese for this recipe is *queso anejo*, a sharp, tangy cheese, that is seldom available here. Freshly grated Parmesan or Romano makes a good substitute.

    4 ears corn, husks removed
    Whipping cream
    Freshly grated Parmesan
    or Romano cheese

1. Place corn in a tightly covered steamer or in a large pot of boiling water. Cook until tender (5 to 7 minutes).

2. Dip the corn in whipping cream, roll in freshly grated cheese, and serve.

Serves 4.

ELOTE CON CREMA
Corn and cream

Elote con crema makes an elegant side dish—it's a tasty combination of corn, tomatoes, onions, and chiles simmered in a rich, satisfying sauce made from half-and-half and cream cheese. Creamed corn was never like this!

    3 tablespoons butter
      Half an onion, chopped
    1 clove garlic, crushed
    2 poblano chiles, roasted,
      peeled, seeded, and cut
      into strips (rajas) or 1 can
      (4 oz) diced green chiles
    1 tomato, chopped
    1½ cups fresh corn kernels
      cut from the cob or 1 package
      (10 oz) frozen corn
    1 package (8 oz) cream
      cheese, cubed
    ½ cup half-and-half
      Salt to taste

1. In a skillet, melt butter and sauté onion and garlic until onion is soft. Add chile rajas and tomato; cook until soft. Add corn and sauté briefly.

2. Reduce heat to low and add cream cheese, stirring until the cheese has softened and begins to melt. Slowly stir in the half-and-half and simmer for 5 minutes. Check seasoning and add salt to taste. Serve immediately.

Serves 4 to 6.

CHAYOTES CON ELOTE Y CHILE
Chayotes with corn and chile

Although chayotes can be served plain—steamed, peeled, cut into bite-sized pieces, and buttered—in this recipe corn and chiles add a pleasant complement of textures and taste to the chayotes.

    3 chayotes
    1 small onion, finely chopped
    1 clove garlic, crushed
    3 tablespoons butter
    2 ears fresh corn kernels
      cut from the cob or 1 package
      (10 oz) frozen corn
    3 large, mild green chiles,
      roasted, peeled, seeded,
      and cut into strips (rajas)
      or 1 can (4 oz) whole green
      chiles, seeded and cut
      into strips
    ½ cup half-and-half
      Salt to taste
    2 tablespoons freshly grated
      Parmesan or Romano cheese

1. Halve chayotes but do not peel; place in a steamer or cover with water in a saucepan; bring to a boil, reduce heat, cover, and cook until fork-tender (approximately 15 minutes). Allow to cool. Peel and cut into bite-sized pieces. (If you peel the chayote before cooking it, it gives off a sticky substance that irritates the skin.)

2. In a large saucepan sauté the onion and garlic in butter until the onion is soft. Add corn and chiles; cook for 5 minutes. Add chayotes and half-and-half and mix gently. Cover and simmer until the corn is tender (approximately 6 minutes). Check the seasoning and add salt to taste if necessary.

3. Top with the freshly grated cheese.

Serves 6.

CHILES RELLENOS
Stuffed chiles

Chiles rellenos is a classic Mexican dish and certainly a favorite in the United States. The chile relleno is a large, mild, green cooking chile that has been roasted, cleaned, and peeled; filled and dipped in batter; and fried until puffed and golden. In Mexico the chile relleno is always served in a sauce. There are three distinct schools of thought on the egg batter in which the chile is dipped: The batter may be flat, fluffy, or extra fluffy. The recipe that follows is right in the middle and the easiest to manage. If you want flatter chiles rellenos, just beat the eggs without separating them. For fluffier chiles rellenos, fold in one tablespoon flour for each egg in the recipe. For directions on how to roast chiles, see page 17.

Although in Mexico the chile relleno is most often filled with a spiced shredded meat mixture, Picadillo (see pages 75-76), in the United States it is usually filled with cheese. In Mexico the cheese-filled chile relleno is identified on menus as "Chile relleno con queso." The chile relleno is usually served as a main dish but it can also be served as a vegetable side dish or as a brunch dish.

A variation of chiles rellenos is chiles en nogada. Chiles en nogada is a classic in its own right and is served traditionally on Mexico's two Independence Days, Cinco de Mayo and the Sixteenth of September.

> 6 *large, mild, green chiles,*
> *roasted and peeled,*
> *leaving on stems (or canned*
> *whole green chiles)*
> ½ *pound jack or Colby cheese,*
> *cut into strips approximately*
> *½ inch wide, 2 inches*
> *long, and ¼ inch thick*
> *Flour*
> 4 *eggs, separated*
> *Oil 1 inch deep, for frying*
> *Sour cream and cilantro,*
> *for garnish*

Tomato Sauce

> 1 *tablespoon oil*
> ½ *cup chopped onion*
> 2 *cloves garlic, crushed*
> 1 *can (28 oz) solid-pack*
> *tomatoes, puréed briefly*
> *in blender*
> 3½ *cups chicken broth*

1. Carefully slit each chile lengthwise along one side; remove seeds and veins. Fill each chile with several strips of cheese, roll in flour, and set aside.

2. Beat egg whites until stiff; slightly beat yolks and fold into whites. Heat oil in a large skillet to 400° F. Drop a large spoonful of the egg mixture into the oil; lay a chile in the middle, top with another spoonful of egg, and smooth the egg to enclose all sides. Carefully baste the top with hot oil, to set. Cook until golden on the underside (about 1 minute); turn and cook again until golden on the underside. Drain on paper towels while preparing Tomato Sauce.

3. Carefully place the rellenos into the tomato sauce and simmer gently to heat thoroughly (about 15 minutes). Do not cook too long or batter will begin to break away.

4. Serve with some of the sauce, and garnish with a dab of sour cream and a few cilantro leaves.

Serves 3 to 6.

Tomato Sauce Heat oil in a large saucepan. Add onion and garlic and cook only until the onion is soft. Add puréed tomatoes and chicken broth, bring to a boil, reduce heat, and simmer 5 minutes.

CHILES EN NOGADA
Stuffed chiles in walnut cream sauce

This dish was developed in celebration of the Independence of Mexico. The colors of the Mexican flag are represented by the white nogada sauce, the green chile and the cilantro garnish, and the red pomegranate seeds.

The nogada is a delicate-flavored walnut cream sauce served cold over a warm chile that has been stuffed with picadillo. For patriotic occasions nuts and pieces of fruit are added to the picadillo.

> 6 *fresh poblano chiles, roasted*
> *and peeled, leaving on stems*
> *Picadillo (see pages 75-76)*
> *Pomegranate seeds and cilan-*
> *tro leaves, for garnish*

Walnut Cream Sauce

> 1 *cup walnuts*
> 1 *cup sour cream*
> ⅔ *cup half-and-half*
> 2 *tablespoons brandy*
> 2 *teaspoons sugar*
> ¼ *teaspoon ground cinnamon*

1. Carefully slit each chile lengthwise along one side; remove seeds and veins. Fill each chile with approximately ½ cup Picadillo, place in a baking pan, and keep warm in a 300° F oven while preparing sauce.

2. To serve, place the warm chiles on individual serving plates, top with approximately ¼ cup cold Walnut Cream Sauce, and garnish with a few pomegranate seeds and cilantro leaves.

Serves 6.

Walnut Cream Sauce Place walnuts in blender, cover, and finely grind. Remove and place in a bowl. Add sour cream, half-and-half, brandy, sugar, and cinnamon; stir until smooth.

COLIFLOR CON SALSA DE JALAPEÑOS ROJOS
Cauliflower with red jalapeño sauce

This recipe combines two vegetables, each with a distinctive taste, in a truly unique side dish. The contrast in color—white cauliflower against red jalapeño sauce—makes this dish a beautiful highlight for any luncheon or dinner menu.

1   large head cauliflower
    Salsa de Jalapeños Rojos
    (see page 22)
1   tablespoon crumbled queso
    fresco or feta cheese

1. Prepare Salsa de Jalapeños Rojos.

2. Break cauliflower into flowerets and steam until tender, about 12 minutes; do not overcook. Arrange the cauliflower in a serving dish and top with the warm Salsa de Jalapeños Rojos.

3. Garnish with the crumbled cheese and serve.

Serves 4 to 6.

The art of dressing up plain vegetables to create something much more special is a hallmark of Mexican cuisine. This dish, cauliflower topped with a jalapeño sauce and crumbled cheese, is striking as well as delicious.

CHILE CON QUESO
Chiles with cheese sauce

Chile con queso is a delicate blending of chiles, tomatoes, and onion in a cheese and cream sauce. Its smooth, creamy texture and savory flavor account for its great popularity throughout the southwestern United States, where it is made with yellow cheese and served as a dip accompanied by Totopos (fried tortilla wedges, see page 62). You may substitute a mild cheddar for the cream cheese if you wish; however, cream cheese makes a more authentic chile con queso.

In Mexico chile con queso is served as an antojito (hors d'oeuvre or snack); as a creamed vegetable side dish to accompany grilled, barbecued, or roasted meats; and as a brunch dish accompanied by frijoles refritos and hot, soft tortillas.

3 tablespoons butter
1 onion, finely chopped
3 tomatoes, peeled and chopped
4 mild green chiles, roasted, peeled, seeded, and torn into strips or 1 can (4 oz) diced green chiles
1 package (8 oz) cream cheese, cut into cubes
½ cup half-and-half

1. In a skillet melt butter over medium heat; add onion and cook until soft. Add tomatoes and chiles and cook until soft.

2. Reduce heat and add the cream cheese, stirring until the cheese is melted. Slowly stir in the half-and-half until mixture is well blended and heated through. Serve warm.

Serves 4 to 6.

CHILES RELLENOS DE ELOTE
Chiles stuffed with fresh corn

Most Americans have only been exposed to chiles rellenos stuffed with cheese. This recipe features a corn and cheese filling typically used in Mexico.

This variation of the chile relleno is a simplified oven-cooking method that may be less intimidating to the novice than the more involved, batter-fried method. It is quick and simple to prepare. Chiles Rellenos de Elote makes a satisfying meatless main dish or a delicious side dish. Serve it with grilled beef, pork, or lamb.

6 large, mild, green chiles, roasted, peeled, and seeded or 2 cans (4 oz each) whole mild green chiles
1 package (10 oz) frozen whole-kernel corn, thawed
2 eggs, lightly beaten
4 tablespoons freshly grated Parmesan or Romano cheese
½ cup half-and-half

1. Preheat oven to 350° F. Slit each chile lengthwise along one side.

2. Purée the corn in a blender or food processor. Mix corn, eggs, and half the cheese together. Fill the prepared chiles with the corn mixture and arrange in a baking dish.

3. Top the chiles with the half-and-half and the remaining cheese. Bake for 25 to 30 minutes.

Serves 4 to 6.

QUELITES
Greens

In Mexico the word *quelites* (greens) covers a variety of plants used for cooked greens that are unknown in most parts of the United States. Many are collected as wild greens and the types of greens available vary in the different regions.

Verdolagas (purslane) is perhaps the most typical of these greens and is sold in the vegetable stands and markets in Mexico. Most of the common greens used in this country can be substituted in this recipe, or you might want to grow your own purslane.

2 pounds greens
1 small onion, chopped
1 clove garlic, minced
1 tablespoon oil
1 mild green chile, roasted, peeled, seeded, and chopped
2 tomatoes, chopped
Garnish: sour cream or crumbled queso fresco or feta cheese

1. Trim off and discard any tough stalk ends and coarsely chop the greens. Place greens in a large pot in a small amount of boiling salted water and cook just until tender (approximately 2 to 4 minutes); drain and set aside.

2. In a large skillet sauté onion and garlic in oil until soft. Add chiles and tomatoes and cook until soft. Add the cooked greens and continue cooking for a few minutes to allow flavors to blend.

3. Garnish with a dab of sour cream or a sprinkling of crumbled cheese.

Serves 4 to 6.

MEZCLA DE VERDURAS CON CHILES
Cabbage succotash

This recipe, with its unusual combination of vegetables, produces a side dish with a multitude of flavors.

> Half a small head of cabbage, sliced
> 3 tablespoons butter
> 1 cup corn, cooked
> 2 poblano chiles, roasted, peeled, seeded, and cut in strips or 1 can (4 oz) whole green chiles, seeded and cut in strips
> 1 tomato, chopped

1. In a large skillet heat butter and sauté cabbage for 5 minutes.

2. Add corn, chiles, and tomato. Cook, stirring, until cabbage is just tender, about 3 minutes.

Serves 4 to 6.

CHICHARITOS A LA MEXICANA
Green peas Mexican style

This is probably one of the most popular vegetable side dishes served in the Mexican home.

> 1 tablespoon butter
> 1 clove garlic, peeled
> Half an onion, chopped
> 1 tomato, chopped
> 1 package (10 oz) frozen small green peas
> 2 tablespoons water

1. In a medium saucepan melt butter and add garlic clove. Allow the garlic to cook until golden. Remove garlic and discard.

2. Sauté onion in the butter until soft; add tomato and cook until soft. Break up the peas and add the peas and water. Bring to a boil, reduce heat, cover, and simmer for 10 minutes.

Serves 4.

CALABACITAS CON QUESO Y CHILES
Zucchini with cheese and green chiles

Every summer many home gardeners find themselves with an abundance of zucchini and a shortage of zucchini recipes. This recipe provides a new way to use zucchini and will be sure to please your family or guests.

> Half an onion, chopped
> 1 clove garlic, minced
> 3 tablespoons butter
> 1 tomato, chopped
> 3 large, mild, green chiles, roasted, peeled, seeded, and chopped or 1 can (4 oz) diced green chiles
> ¼ teaspoon dried oregano
> 3 tablespoons water
> 1 pound zucchini, cut into ½-inch slices
> ⅓ cup grated jack cheese

1. In a large skillet sauté onion and garlic in butter until soft. Add tomato, chiles, and oregano and cook until the tomato is soft. Stir the water into the vegetables and add the zucchini. Cover and cook until the squash is tender.

2. Sprinkle the cheese over the vegetables, cover, and cook only until the cheese has melted. Gently stir, taking care not to mash the zucchini. Serve immediately.

Serves 4 to 6.

PLÁTANOS
Plantains, cooking bananas

Bananas are available in great variety in Mexico—yellow, red, black, long, fat, and short. The cooking bananas are becoming increasingly available in our markets. Generally fatter than the common banana, they may be marketed from their green stage through yellow to black. The green ones ripen quickly in a warm room and are ready to cook when black and soft to the touch. Common bananas may be substituted in these recipes, but should be used before they are fully ripe.

PLÁTANOS FRITOS
Fried bananas

The *plátano* (plantain) is a fruit—the cooking banana of Mexico. This dish is unusual because the fruit is served as a vegetable. Similar to french-fried potatoes, it makes a unique side dish or snack. If plantains are available, choose ones with black skins that are soft to the touch. If plantains are unavailable, select regular bananas that are not yet ripe.

> 3 plantains or unripe bananas
> ½ cup butter
> Salt

1. Peel plantains and slice crosswise in ½-inch-thick slices.

2. Melt half the butter in a skillet. Sauté the plantain slices, a few at a time, until tender and golden brown. Add more butter as needed. Salt lightly and serve.

Serves 6.

Velvety rich black beans make a striking side dish. They are a staple in Mexican cooking, and for good reason: They are both delicious and nutritious.

FRIJOLES
Beans

Beans are a staple in Mexican cuisine. There is no doubt that they are, at the very least, "daily fare" and provide an important part of the nutrition in the diet of Mexico.

Beans are offered in great variety in Mexican markets and one sometimes wonders whether vendors choose them for their range of color as well as for their range of flavors and cooking characteristics. In the large city markets, each bean merchant will display baskets with as many as fifteen or twenty varieties. Rural markets will have only half that many, depending upon regional availability and preference. Your own choice of beans is likely to include only pinto and black beans.

Although other vegetables in the Mexican cuisine are seldom served unembellished, frijoles are the exception. Traditionally they are cooked and served plain, as in frijoles de olla, and frijoles refritos.

FRIJOLES NEGROS
Black beans

Black beans are used more frequently in the southern regions of Mexico. They are cooked with a sprig of fresh epazote, which adds a subtle flavor characteristic of the herb. There is no substitute for epazote so if it is unavailable simply omit; the beans will be delicious even without it.

> 2 cups black beans
> 8 cups water
> 2 tablespoons lard or oil
> 2 teaspoons salt
> 2 sprigs fresh epazote, if available
> Garnishes (optional): sour cream, minced onion, slices of jalapeño

1. Pick through and wash the beans. Do not soak.

2. Place beans, water, and lard in a large pot. Bring to a boil, reduce heat, cover, and simmer until the skins have begun to split (about 2 hours). Add salt and epazote (if used) and continue to cook for another hour, or until very tender.

3. Serve in small bowls. Garnish if desired.

Makes approximately 6 cups cooked beans.

FRIJOLES DE OLLA
Beans from the pot

Here is the bean in its simplest and finest form. The long, slow cooking allows the flavor of the beans to reach its fullest.

In Mexico soaking beans overnight is considered undesirable. Beans should be cooked slowly with nothing more than water, lard, and salt—the salt being added only after the beans are tender and the skins have begun to split. This prevents the beans from becoming tough. Cooked beans improve in flavor after a day or two, but of course must be refrigerated.

> 2 cups dry pinto beans
> 8 to 10 cups water
> 2 tablespoons lard or oil
> 2 teaspoons salt, or to taste
> Garnishes (optional): salsa, minced onion, sour cream, and grated or crumbled cheese

1. Pick through and wash the beans. Do not soak.

2. Place beans, water, and lard in a large pot. Bring to a boil, reduce heat, cover, and simmer until the skins have begun to split (2 to 2½ hours). Add the salt and continue to cook until the beans are very tender (about 30 minutes longer).

3. Serve in small bowls. Garnish if desired.

Makes approximately 6 cups cooked beans.

FRIJOLES REFRITOS
Well-fried beans

Frijoles refritos is usually translated as "refried beans," which is a misleading interpretation. The "re" of refritos does not refer to a second or repeated cooking but rather indicates that the beans have been fried properly or "well-fried."

Frijoles refritos is a classic side dish and it is commonly served daily in the Mexican home. There is always a pot of frijoles de olla ready and waiting; beans are taken from the pot and freshly fried for the meal.

The ground avocado leaf is not a necessary ingredient in this dish; however, it is used in some regions of Mexico and is an interesting flavor.

> ¼ cup lard or oil
> 4 to 5 cups cooked pinto or black beans, drained, reserving the broth
> 1 clove garlic, crushed
> Garnish (optional): crumbled quesco fresco or ground avocado leaf

1. In a large heavy skillet, heat the lard until hot enough for a bean to sizzle when placed in it. Reduce the heat and add 1 cup beans and mash thoroughly. Add garlic and stir.

2. Add the remaining beans, approximately 1 cup at a time, mashing thoroughly after each addition. Reduce heat and allow the beans to cook into a thick paste. If too dry, stir in small amounts of the reserved bean broth.

3. If using ground avocado leaf, lightly toast the fresh or dried leaf on a preheated heavy frying pan or comal. Grind into a fine powder.

4. Serve the beans garnished with crumbled queso fresco or a sprinkling of the ground avocado leaf.

Serves 6.

Masa is the mainstay of Mexican cuisine. It is used to make the tortilla, which accompanies nearly every meal, and is found in many other dishes as well.

Masa Dishes

The tortilla and other dishes made from *masa* (a special dough ground from lime-treated corn kernels) were the heart of ancient Mexican cuisine. Today corn dishes remain the mainstay of contemporary Mexican cooking. Corn cookery in Mexico uses techniques with origins as lost in prehistory as the origins of corn itself. Featured here are techniques for making your own corn and flour tortillas in the traditional manner, as well as recipes for tacos, enchiladas, flautas, tamales, and more.

MASA

The word *masa* literally translates as "dough," but in Mexico masa means, specifically, the fresh corn dough used for tortillas and other corn dishes. Not merely the bread of Mexico, the tortilla is often the plate and spoon as well. This simple, unleavened disk lends itself to all manner of uses. It is folded over some fillings and rolled around others; it can be fried or toasted to serve as a scoop, or dried and broken up to form the base for casseroles and thickening for soups or sauces.

To make tortillas you must have masa and masa is made from *nixtamal*. Nixtamal is dried white field corn that is cooked and lime-soaked for many hours. Blue corn masa dishes, which are popular in some regions of Mexico and in the southwestern United States, are simply made from blue field corn instead of the more common white corn.

With the hulls removed the corn is rinsed numerous times and then ground into the fresh dough known as masa. This fresh masa is used plain to make corn tortillas. With the addition of other ingredients it is used to make tamales or other masa dishes. Masa harina is a "flour" made from fresh masa that has been dehydrated. Fortunately, masa harina is available throughout the United States. Although tortillas and other masa dishes made from masa harina are not quite the same as those made from fresh masa, there is much to be said for the convenience and availability of this product. However, there are many ethnic shopping areas in the United States where fresh masa can be purchased and, of course, fresh tortillas are available in markets throughout the country.

Traditionally the nixtamal was ground into masa by hand on the *metate* and *mano* (grinding stone). Today the production of masa and of tortillas has been almost completely mechanized, although hand-patted tortillas are still made and sold at higher prices. Even in remote villages, the grinding of the nixtamal into masa is generally done with a hand-cranked Corona-type mill, rather than with the metate, and a tortilla press often replaces the 30 to 40 pats that a good tortilla maker needs to shape a tortilla from a ball of masa. The metate and mano have by no means been retired. Even though they are seldom used to initially grind the masa, they are still used to "silken" the dough (a brief working of the masa) just before making the tortillas, tamales, or other masa dishes.

If you wonder why this complex process is still used in preference to dry grinding, just try eating tortillas made from cornmeal that is dry-ground. In contrast, the lime-treated corn, ground into fresh dough, gives a texture and flavor that can't be approached by dry-grinding.

TORTILLAS DE MAIZ
Corn tortillas

The corn tortilla is without question the mainstay of the diet of Mexico. In many restaurants in Mexico, you can watch as the tortillas are made to order using the age-old, traditional hand-patted technique.

> 2 cups masa harina
> 1¼ cups warm water, or more
>   if needed

1. Place the masa harina in a bowl. Gradually work the water into the masa harina. Mix together well. Knead for 3 to 5 minutes, pushing hard with the heel of your hand. Keep the dough wrapped in waxed paper or plastic wrap while you make the tortillas, so that it does not dry out.

2. Heat a heavy frying pan over medium-high heat. Break off a walnut-sized piece of dough and hand-pat it 2 or 3 times to partially flatten. Place on a tortilla press between two pieces of plastic wrap or waxed paper. Close the lid and press. Remove the tortilla and peel the plastic away from the tortilla. If you don't have a press, a rolling pin may be used; however, the dough must still be placed between pieces of plastic wrap or waxed paper or it will stick to the rolling pin.

3. Place the tortilla on the heated, ungreased heavy frying pan. Cook until the edges begin to dry (about 30 seconds). Turn over and bake until lightly speckled on the underside (about 1 minute). Turn a second time and bake for an additional 30 seconds. (The side that is now facing up is meant to be the face of the tortilla, the side on which the filling is placed.) The total cooking time will be between 2 and 3 minutes, depending upon the thickness of the tortilla and the temperature of the pan. A well-made tortilla will usually puff up on the second flip, so don't be alarmed when this happens.

4. Wrap the tortillas together in a cloth as they are made, to keep them soft and warm.

Makes 1 dozen tortillas.

<u>Cooking Notes</u> If you have the correct amount of liquid in the dough, the plastic will easily peel away from the tortilla. If the dough cracks at the edges, add a little more water and knead well. If the tortilla sticks to the plastic, add a little more masa harina to the dough and knead well. It takes a little practice to know how the dough should feel.

TORTILLAS DE HARINA
Flour tortillas

The flour tortilla is a variation of the traditional corn tortilla but is common only in northern Mexico, which is the wheat-growing region. Flour tortillas are also popular in the southwestern United States. Wheat flour is called *harina de trigo* and dough made from the flour is called *masa de trigo.*

In the state of Sonora, Mexico, many Sonorans pride themselves on their paper-thin flour tortillas. Sometimes they are as much as 2 feet across and so thin that you can see the outlines of your fingers through them. For regular use, flour tortillas are generally made a little larger than corn tortillas. Don't get discouraged if your first efforts are ragged and uneven.

> 2 cups flour
> 1 teaspoon salt (scant)
> ½ teaspoon baking powder
> ¼ cup lard or shortening
> ½ cup warm water

1. Mix together flour, salt, and baking powder. Cut in the lard and mix well. Gradually add the water, working it in to make a stiff dough. Knead until the dough is springy. Divide the dough into balls of equal size; cover and allow to rest for 20 to 30 minutes.

2. Heat a comal or heavy frying pan over medium-high heat. On a lightly floured board, use a rolling pin to roll each dough ball into a thin circle approximately 8 inches across.

3. Place the tortilla on the heated, ungreased comal. Bake until speckled with brown (1½ to 2 minutes); turn over and bake until the underside is speckled brown (1½ to 2 minutes). The tortilla may puff up while cooking; if so, press down lightly with a linen towel.

4. Wrap the tortillas together in a kitchen towel as they are made to keep them soft and warm.

Makes 1 dozen flour tortillas.

Step-by-step

HOW TO MAKE CORN AND FLOUR TORTILLAS

The process of making corn tortillas is somewhat different from that of making flour tortillas. Corn tortillas are flattened in a press, while flour tortillas are rolled out. Below, we show you some of the steps involved in making each.

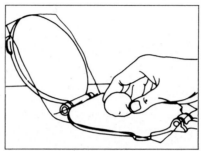

1. To shape corn tortillas: Put a piece of waxed paper on the surface of the tortilla press. Place a walnut-sized piece of masa slightly back of center on the press. Place a piece of waxed paper on top of the ball of dough and then take the handle of the press and press down hard to flatten the masa.

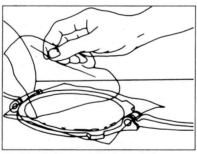

2. Open the press to reveal the flattened dough. Remove the waxed paper from the tortilla and then lift off the tortilla.

3. To make flour tortillas: After kneading, make balls of dough by squeezing a handful of dough so that a small ball of it extrudes from your fist. After balls are made, lightly coat each one with lard and place in a bowl.

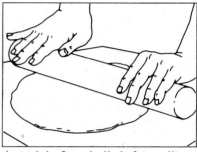

4. Lightly flour balls before rolling. Roll once forward and once back.

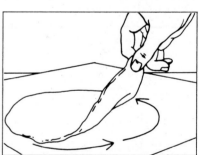

5. Flip tortilla and revolve a quarter turn. Keep rolling until desired size and thickness is achieved.

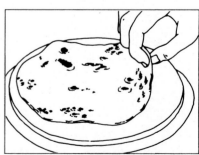

6. Both corn and flour tortillas are baked on a hot, ungreased comal. Cook on both sides until speckled brown and cooked through.

TACOS

In this country most people think of a taco as a folded, crisply fried tortilla, filled with meat, cheese, lettuce, and anything else handy. In Mexico, however, it takes a lot of looking to find a crisply fried taco.

The most typical taco in Mexico is made with a soft, unfried corn tortilla that is filled and garnished, often with nothing more than salsa, although the range of possible fillings and garnishes is endless. A soft, fried taco shell is also served in Mexico. This is a corn tortilla fried briefly only until it is soft.

In this recipe, three methods for cooking the taco shell will be given: the soft, unfried shell preferred in Mexico; the soft, briefly fried shell; and the crisply fried taco shell that is served in the United States.

Corn tortillas
Oil ¼ to ½ inch deep, for frying tortillas (optional)
Choice of filling (see Note)
Any combination or all of these garnishes: sour cream, sliced avocado or guacamole, salsa, minced onion, chopped tomato, shredded lettuce, crumbled queso fresco or grated cheese

Traditional Method

1. Preheat a heavy frying pan over high heat. The pan is sufficiently hot when a drop of water "dances" when dropped onto the heated surface.

2. Dampen your hands with water and rub the tortilla to moisten it. Cook over high heat, turning once. The tortilla should be soft. The tortillas may be kept soft and warm by wrapping them, as they are cooked, in a slightly dampened towel and placing them in a 200° F oven until the remaining tortillas are cooked.

3. Fill, fold, and serve immediately, allowing each person to garnish as desired.

Briefly Fried Method

1. Pour oil into a skillet to a depth of ¼ inch. Heat to 400° to 425° F. (Oil is sufficiently hot when a tiny bit of tortilla dropped into it pops immediately to the surface.) Fry the tortillas, one at a time, just long enough to soften them (a few seconds on each side). Drain on paper towels.

2. Fill and fold. The tacos may be stacked together side by side in a foil-lined baking pan. Cover tightly with foil and keep warm in a 300° F oven as each taco is made. Serve immediately, allowing each person to garnish as desired.

Crisply Fried Method

1. Pour oil into a skillet to a depth of ½ inch. Heat over high heat to 400° to 425° F. (Oil is sufficiently hot when a tiny bit of tortilla dropped into it pops immediately to the surface.)

2. Fold the tortilla in half, holding the top edges together with tongs. Briefly press the center of the tortilla to the bottom of the skillet to flatten and set. Turn the tortilla on its side and cook, holding the upper side with tongs to prevent the edges from sticking together. Cook until golden and crisp; turn over and repeat on the other side. Drain on paper towels.

3. Fill with prepared filling. The tortillas may be stacked together side by side in a baking pan and held in a 300° F oven, covered, while the remaining tacos are fried.

4. Serve immediately, allowing each person to garnish as desired.

Cooking Notes Use only corn tortillas for tacos. Freshly made corn tortillas do not fry well; use tortillas that are at least one day old.

Any of the recipes in the "Fillings" section of this chapter, except for the queso (cheese) fillings, may be used for tacos. However, the most commonly used and perhaps the best choices would be Res (see page 75), Carnitas (see page 86), Chorizo (see page 88), Puerco (see page 76), Birria (see page 89), Pollo (see page 77), and Pescado (see page 77).

TAQUITOS
Miniature tacos

Taquitos are miniature tacos and are particularly good to serve for an antojito (hors d'oeuvres) buffet. Any of the fillings used for tacos may be used for taquitos. A favorite choice for these little miniatures, however, is the Camaron filling (see page 77).

1. Using a 2-inch round biscuit cutter, cut circles from corn tortillas; follow the recipe for Tacos (see page 58).

2. Prepare all of the taquitos, fill, garnish, and arrange on a serving platter.

Homemade tortillas are much more flavorful than storebought ones, plus they are fun to make. Flour tortillas are shaped by rolling, while corn tortillas are flattened in a tortilla press. Both types are then cooked on a hot comal or in a skillet.

59

TOSTADAS

Tostadas are corn tortillas fried flat and crisp and then topped with frijoles refritos (refried beans) and perhaps some shredded meat. Garnished with a variety of ingredients, a tostada becomes a whole meal on an edible plate. Use corn tortillas that are at least one day old because fresh corn tortillas do not fry well.

> *Oil ¼ inch deep, for frying*
> *Day-old corn tortillas*
> *Salt*
> *Frijoles Refritos (see page 53)*
> *Shredded meat (optional; see page 73)*
> *Garnishes: sour cream, sliced avocado or guacamole, salsa, chopped tomato, shredded lettuce, radish slices, whole ripe olives, and crumbled queso fresco or grated cheese*

1. Heat oil in a skillet over high heat to 400° F to 425° F. (Oil is sufficiently hot when a tiny bit of tortilla dropped into it pops immediately to the surface.) Lightly salt the tortillas and cook them one at a time, turning once, until golden brown and crisp. Drain on paper towels. The tostada shells may be kept warm in a 300° F oven.

2. Spread each tostada shell with a layer of frijoles refritos. Top with shredded meat, if desired.

3. Garnish and serve.

TOSTADITAS
Miniature tostadas

Tostaditas—miniature tostadas—are also good to serve for an antojito (hors d'oeuvres) buffet.

1. Using a 2-inch round biscuit cutter, cut circles from corn tortillas; follow the recipe for Tostadas (see above).

2. Prepare all of the tostaditas, garnish, and arrange on a serving platter.

EMPANADAS
Turnovers

Although not really a masa dish, the *empanada* seems to fall into the masa category best. The empanada is common to all Hispanic countries. Brought to the New World by the Spanish, it has spread to many countries and assumed many forms, from small appetizer empanaditas to medium-sized dessert empanadas (see page 121) to an *empanada gallega*, a large pie stuffed with seafood or meat and vegetables and served hot or cold in slices.

The dough for the empanada can be anything from an elegant, flaky pastry to a bread-type dough that will "stick to the ribs." In Mexico the empanada is a true turnover rather than a pie. Empanada fillings encourage the cook's ingenuity and inventiveness. Almost anything is fair game, including game. In Vera Cruz, a common filling is shrimp, but almost any kind of seafood can be used. Picadillo is commonly used, as is chorizo. In fact, any of the fillings in the section entitled "The Fillings" (pages 73 to 77) except the queso (cheese) fillings may be used in empanadas. Empanadas make excellent picnic fare and are a good way to use up leftovers.

> 2 cups flour
> ¾ cup cold butter, cut into small pieces
> 1 egg, separated
> ¼ cup ice water
> 1½ cups filling of choice (see pages 73–77)

1. Place flour into a large bowl and cut in butter with a pastry blender. In a separate bowl beat together egg yolk and water. Add gradually to the flour mixture and mix until dough forms a cohesive ball. Divide the dough in half for easier handling and turn onto a lightly floured board. Roll out thin. Cut into 7-inch circles.

2. Fill each circle with approximately 3 tablespoons filling. Fold the circle in half, pinch the edge to seal, and flute the edge as for a pie crust. Place on an ungreased baking sheet, brush the tops with the egg white, and bake in a 400° F oven until golden (about 20 minutes).
Makes 8 empanadas.

Note Empanadas make excellent appetizers or hors d'oeuvres. Cut the pastry into 2- or 3-inch circles, fill with approximately 1 tablespoon filling, and bake until golden.
Makes 24 to 30 appetizers.

TORTAS
French roll-type sandwiches

Tortas (as with empanadas) are not really a masa dish but they too seem to fall into this category best. A torta is a sandwich made with the *bolillo*, the Mexican dinner roll that is somewhat like a hard-crusted French dinner roll. These rolls are filled with a warm shredded meat filling and garnished with salsa and shredded lettuce. Any of the fillings in the section entitled "The Fillings" (see pages 73 to 77) may be used for tortas, except the queso (cheese) fillings. Pollo con Tomatillos (see page 76) or Pescado (see page 77) are especially nice in tortas. Tortas are an excellent way to make use of leftovers. Try them also for a picnic.

> *French rolls*
> *Choice of filling, warmed (see pages 73–77)*
> *Salsa, sliced avocado, and radishes*
> *Shredded lettuce*

1. Cut the rolls in half lengthwise and remove part of the bread from the center of the rolls.

2. Fill the bottom half of each roll with the warm prepared filling; top with salsa, sliced avocado, radishes and lettuce. Cover with the top half of the roll and serve.

FLAUTAS

Flautas, meaning "flutes," are rolled corn tortillas that are filled and then fried. (Use corn tortillas that are at least one day old because freshly made corn tortillas do not fry well.) Often two tortillas are overlapped for extra strength and length, although this is not easy to manage. Flautas are usually filled with shredded chicken, beef, or pork and then garnished with guacamole and served on a bed of shredded lettuce. Flautas may be made in advance and reheated in a 350° F oven for 10 to 15 minutes. They freeze well. Thaw and reheat as above.

> 2 *dozen day-old corn tortillas*
> 3 *cups Shredded Beef, Chicken, or Pork (see pages 73–77); Res (see page 75); Carnitas (see page 86); or Pollo con Tomatillos (see page 76)*
> *Oil ½ inch deep, for frying*
> *Salt*
> *Shredded lettuce*
> *Guacamole (see page 40)*
> *Salsa Verde (see page 22) or Salsa de Chipotle (see page 22)*
> *Crumbled queso fresco or sour cream*

1. Preheat a heavy frying pan or comal over high heat. The pan is sufficiently hot when a drop of water dances when dropped onto the heated surface. Dampen your hands with water and rub the tortilla. Cook briefly, turning once, only long enough to soften the tortilla.

2. Fill the tortilla with approximately 2 tablespoons of the prepared shredded meat. Roll tightly and secure with a toothpick. Set aside and cook and fill the next tortilla.

3. Heat the oil in a skillet over high heat to 400° to 425° F. (Oil is sufficiently hot when a tiny bit of tortilla dropped into it pops immediately to the surface.) Lightly salt the flautas and fry, several at a time, until golden and crisp. Drain on paper towels and remove the toothpicks. The flautas may be placed in a baking pan and kept warm in a 300° F oven while the remaining flautas are fried.

4. Mound lettuce on a large platter or divide among individual plates. Arrange flautas (allowing 2 or 3 per serving) over lettuce. Top with guacamole and garnish with salsa and the crumbled queso fresco or a dab of sour cream.

Makes 2 dozen flautas.

Crisp corn tortillas filled with shredded beef filling and topped with avocado and cheese make great flautas. Flautas can also be filled with pork and chicken. Here you see them served with a salad of oranges and pomegranate seeds and Sangría (page 124).

61

BURRITOS

Burritos are made with flour tortillas that are filled and then rolled into a tubular shape. They are common to the northern, wheat-growing region of Mexico. Any of the recipes in the section entitled "The Fillings" (see pages 73 to 77), except for the queso (cheese) fillings, may be used for burritos. The best choices would be: Res (see page 75), Chile Colorado (see page 81), Carnitas (see page 86), Chile Verde (see page 80), Chorizo (see page 88), Birria (see page 89), Pollo con Tomatillos (see page 76), and Pescado (see page 77). It is common for the filling to include frijoles refritos or arroz (rice) in addition to the meat.

> *Flour tortillas*
> *Choice of filling (see suggestions above)*
> *Frijoles Refritos (see page 53) or Arroz (see page 35) (optional)*
> *Any combination or all of these garnishes: salsa, avocado slices or guacamole, chopped onion, sour cream, or grated cheese*

1. Preheat a heavy frying pan or comal over high heat. The pan is sufficiently hot when a drop of water dances when dropped onto the heated surface. Reduce the heat slightly before cooking the flour tortillas.

2. Dampen your hands with water and rub the tortilla. Cook briefly, turning once, only long enough to soften the tortilla. Fill the tortilla with several spoonfuls of the prepared filling; add a spoonful of frijoles refritos or arroz, if desired. Roll one side of the tortilla toward the center, fold a small portion on each end toward the center, and continue to roll the tortilla. The burritos may be placed in a foil-lined baking pan, covered tightly with foil, and held in a 300° F oven while the remaining burritos are assembled.

3. Serve immediately, allowing each person to garnish as desired.

Note Burritos may be made in advance. When ready to serve, tightly wrap each burrito in foil and reheat in a 300° F oven for 10 to 15 minutes.

CHIMICHANGAS
Fried burritos

Chimichangas are burritos that are fried after being filled. They are a "border food," a dish created in the southwestern United States bordering Mexico, and are not typical to the Mexican cuisine. Any of the recipes in the section entitled "The Fillings," except for the queso (cheese) fillings, may be used for chimichangas; however, as with burritos, the best choices are Res (see page 75), Chile Colorado (see page 81), Carnitas (see page 86), Chile Verde (see page 80), Chorizo (see page 88), Birria (see page 89), Pollo con Tomatillos (see page 76), and Pescado (see page 77). The addition of frijoles refritos or arroz in the filling is typical but optional. Chimichangas are an excellent way to use up leftovers.

> *Flour tortillas*
> *Choice of filling (see suggestions above)*
> *Frijoles Refritos (see page 53) or Arroz (see pages 35–37) (optional)*
> *Oil ½ inch deep, for frying*
> *Any combination or all of these garnishes: salsa, avocado slices or guacamole, sour cream, radish rosettes, and whole ripe olives*

1. Follow the instructions for making Burritos (at left), steps 1 and 2.

2. Heat the oil in a skillet over high heat to 400° to 425° F. (Oil is sufficiently hot when a tiny bit of tortilla dropped into it pops immediately to the surface.) Secure each filled, rolled burrito with a toothpick and fry, one at a time, turning once. Cook until golden and crisp. Drain

on paper towels. Each chimichanga may be placed in a baking pan and held in a 300° F oven while the remaining chimichangas are being fried.

3. Remove toothpicks. Garnish as desired and serve.

Note Chimichangas may be made in advance and reheated in a 350° F oven in a baking dish covered with foil for 15 to 20 minutes. They freeze well. Thaw and reheat.

TOTOPOS
Tortilla chips

Totopos are triangular pieces of corn tortillas, fried crisp. We know them in the United States as tortilla chips. They are served as accompaniments to salsa or dips and have become popular in this country served with melted cheese and chile in an appetizer called nachos. Use tortillas that are at least one day old because freshly made corn tortillas do not fry well.

> *Day-old corn tortillas*
> *Oil ¼ inch deep, for frying*
> *Salt*

1. Cut the tortillas into wedges (triangles) by stacking together flat and cutting into sixths, as if cutting a pie.

2. Heat the oil in a skillet over high heat to 400° to 425° F. (Oil is sufficiently hot when a tiny bit of tortilla dropped into it pops immediately to the surface.) Lightly salt the wedges and fry by placing only as many as will fit in a single layer into the skillet at one time. Cook until golden and crisp, turning once. Drain on paper towels.

3. Serve with Salsa (see page 21) or Chile con Queso (see page 50) or as "scoops" to accompany frijoles refritos or shredded meats.

Note Totopos may be prepared in advance and reheated in a 350° F oven.

QUESADILLAS

In the southwestern United States, the *quesadilla* is a corn or flour tortilla folded over a filling of cheese and perhaps chiles, then fried lightly in a skillet. In Mexico the traditional quesadilla is made by filling a small, uncooked tortilla with any of a great variety of fillings, folding and pinching the edges together, and frying. In its simplest form, the quesadilla is the Mexican equivalent of a toasted cheese sandwich—a tortilla filled with cheese, folded, and toasted on an ungreased comal or lightly fried in butter. Either corn or flour tortillas may be used; however, in the southwestern United States, flour tortillas are preferred.

> *Corn or flour tortillas*
> *Fresh nopales (cactus), cleaned and sliced in half lengthwise, or mild green chiles, roasted, peeled, seeded, and opened flat or canned whole green chiles, rinsed, seeded, and opened flat*
> *Sliced jack, Colby, or mild Cheddar cheese (2 slices per serving)*
> *3 tablespoons butter (optional)*
> *Sour cream and salsa or sliced jalapeño, for garnish (optional)*

1. Preheat a heavy frying pan or comal over medium heat. Dampen your hands with water and rub the tortilla. Place in the pan briefly to soften, turn, place the cactus on one half of the tortilla, top with the cheese slices, and fold the tortilla in half.

2. Gently toast the tortilla on both sides until the nopal is tender and the cheese is melted. If you wish to cook the quesadilla in butter, melt the butter in a skillet over medium heat,
add the quesadillas one at a time, and gently toast on both sides until the cheese is melted. The quesadillas may be placed in a foil-lined baking pan, covered tightly with foil (do not cover if toasted in butter), and held in a 300° F oven while the remaining quesadillas are being assembled.

3. Serve immediately, allowing each person to garnish if desired by opening the quesadilla and adding a dab of sour cream and salsa or sliced jalapeño.

QUESADILLA MINIATURES

These little deep-fried quesadilla miniatures are excellent for a party or as an appetizer or snack.

> 2 *cups masa harina*
> 2 *tablespoons flour*
> ½ *teaspoon each baking powder and salt*
> 2 *tablespoons melted butter*
> 1 *egg, lightly beaten*
> ½ *cup milk*
> ¼ *cup freshly grated Romano or Parmesan cheese*

1. Mix together the masa harina, flour, baking powder, and salt. Add butter and egg and mix well. Gradually add milk, using only enough to make a fairly stiff dough. Mix in the cheese. Form the dough into small walnut-sized balls or rolls.

2. Heat oil in a skillet over medium-high heat to 400° F. Oil is sufficiently hot when a tiny bit of masa dropped into it pops immediately to the surface. Fry the masa pieces several at a time until golden. Drain on paper towels. The quesadillas may be placed in a baking pan and held in a 300° F oven while the remaining balls are being fried. They may be made in advance and reheated in a 350° F oven, covered, for 10 to 15 minutes.

3. Serve warm.

Makes 3 to 4 dozen quesadilla miniatures.

TRADITIONAL QUESADILLAS

The most traditional quesadilla served in Mexico is a turnover made of masa (rather than a precooked tortilla), with a filling that usually includes cheese and may include meat or beans as well. Any of the fillings in the section entitled "The Fillings" (pages 73 to 77) may be used.

> 2 *cups masa harina*
> 2 *tablespoons flour*
> ½ *teaspoon each baking powder and salt*
> 2 *tablespoons melted butter*
> 1 *egg, lightly beaten*
> ½ *cup milk*
> ¾ *cup filling, any type*
> *Oil ¼ inch deep, for frying*

1. Mix together the masa harina, flour, baking powder, and salt. Add butter and egg and mix well. Gradually add milk, using only enough to make a fairly stiff dough.

2. Using a tortilla press lined with plastic wrap, form small tortillas 3 to 4 inches across. Place approximately 1 tablespoon of the prepared filling in the center of each tortilla. Fold in half and pinch the edges to seal.

3. Heat oil in a skillet over high heat to 400° F. (Oil is sufficiently hot when a tiny bit of masa dropped into it pops immediately to the surface.) Fry the quesadillas several at a time until golden. Drain on paper towels. The quesadillas may be placed in a baking pan and held in a 300° F oven while the remaining quesadillas are being fried.

4. Serve immediately.

Makes 1 dozen quesadillas.

ENCHILADAS

Enchiladas are "chilied" tortillas. Behind that simple definition there is probably the greatest variety of dishes that come under one name in Mexican cooking.

There are many wonderful enchilada sauces, some specific to certain regions in Mexico. In northern Mexico and the American Southwest, enchiladas made with a red chile sauce (Enchiladas Coloradas: see recipe at right) are most common. From Mexico City south, the distinctive mole sauce is more common (see Enchiladas de Mole, pages 66 and 67).

Like so many other seemingly complicated dishes, enchiladas are quite easy to make if you're organized. If the ingredients are properly laid out, it takes little more time to make 60 for a party than it does to make a dozen. For speed and efficiency, set up a production line. Have ready the corn tortillas; a skillet with heated oil; a second skillet with the prepared, heated sauce; a large, empty plate on which to fill and roll the enchiladas; bowls with the filling ingredients (cheese, meat, onion, olives, or other ingredients); and, finally, the baking dish into which the rolled enchiladas will be placed for baking.

Enchiladas may be rolled, stacked, or folded. Variations in fillings, sauces, and garnishes offer endless combinations of tastes. Authentic enchiladas are always made with corn tortillas.

ENCHILADAS COLORADAS
Red enchiladas

This red enchilada sauce is made in the traditional manner and is most commonly used in northern Mexico and the southwestern United States. It is not typical in Mexico to thicken a cooking sauce with flour; however, this sauce is the exception, as it comes from the wheat-growing region.

Sauce

    3   dried ancho chiles
    3   dried California chiles
    2   pasilla chiles, if available
    3   cups water
    2   cloves garlic, chopped
    1   teaspoon salt
    1   teaspoon dried oregano
    ½   teaspoon ground cumin
    ¼   teaspoon ground cloves
    3   tablespoons lard or oil
    2   tablespoons flour
    3½ cups liquid (liquid from
        the chiles plus chicken broth
        to make 3½ cups)

Filling

Have prepared one recipe of any of the following fillings:

    Res (see page 75)
    Queso y Cebolla (see page 77)
    Chorizo (see page 88)
    Pescado (see page 77)

To Assemble

    1   dozen corn tortillas
        Oil ¼ inch deep, for frying
    ¼   pound longhorn, Colby,
        or jack cheese, grated
        Garnishes: Sour cream,
        chopped green onion, cilantro,
        and whole ripe olives

1. *To prepare the sauce:* Remove the stems and seeds from the chiles and discard. Place the chiles in a saucepan with the water. Bring to a boil, reduce heat to medium, and cook for 5 minutes. Set aside to steep for 30 minutes.

2. Drain the chiles, reserving the liquid. Scrape the pulp from any tough pieces of skin. Discard the skin. Place chiles in a blender or food processer together with the garlic, salt, oregano, cumin, and cloves. Blend to a smooth purée. If a smoother-textured sauce is desired, strain the purée.

3. In a skillet heat the lard, add flour, and lightly sauté, stirring. Add the chile purée and fry for 3 minutes, stirring constantly. Measure the liquid reserved from the chiles and add chicken broth to measure a total of 3½ cups. Slowly stir in the liquid. Bring to a boil, stirring constantly. Reduce heat and simmer 5 minutes. Keep warm.

4. *To assemble enchiladas:* Preheat oven to 350° F. Heat oil in a skillet over high heat to 400° to 425° F. (Oil is sufficiently hot when a tiny bit of tortilla dropped into it pops immediately to the surface.) Fry each tortilla, one at a time, only long enough to soften it (a few seconds per side). Lift the tortilla with tongs and move it into the warm sauce. Turn to coat both sides of tortilla; then lift to a plate. Place some of the prepared filling across the middle of the tortilla, roll, and place seam side down in a baking pan. Repeat until all tortillas are filled and rolled.

5. Spoon a small amount of the remaining sauce across the length of each enchilada, paying particular attention to coat the ends. Sprinkle the grated cheese over the enchiladas, cover the pan tightly with foil, and bake until enchiladas are heated through and cheese has melted (20 to 30 minutes).

6. Garnish enchiladas before serving.

Makes 1 dozen enchiladas.

Note This sauce freezes well and is a tremendous convenience when prepared ahead and frozen. Make a large quantity; it will keep successfully up to one year in the freezer. To prepare the sauce for freezing, follow steps 1 and 2 in the instructions. Divide the chile purée into quantities for making a single recipe and freeze. When ready to make Enchiladas Coloradas, thaw the chile purée and proceed with step 3. Then continue to assemble the enchiladas.

ENCHILADAS COLORADAS II
Red enchiladas

This is a simplified version of the traditional sauce for Enchiladas Coloradas. Use this recipe as a convenient timesaver for the sauce portion of that recipe, then proceed with the ingredients and instructions in the main recipe (see opposite page).

    1 can (6 oz) tomato sauce
    2 cloves garlic, chopped
    1 teaspoon dried oregano
    ½ teaspoon ground cumin
    ¼ teaspoon ground cloves
    3 tablespoons lard or oil
    1 tablespoon flour
    1 can (10 oz) red chile sauce
    ½ teaspoon salt, if necessary

1. Place the tomato sauce, garlic, oregano, cumin, and cloves in a blender or food processor, and blend briefly.

2. In a skillet heat the lard over medium heat, add flour, and lightly sauté, stirring. Add the tomato purée and fry for 3 minutes, stirring constantly. Slowly stir in the red chile sauce. Bring to a boil, stirring constantly; reduce heat and simmer 5 minutes. Keep warm.

3. To assemble the enchiladas see recipe for Enchiladas Coloradas, page 64, steps 4 through 6.

ENCHILADAS SONORA
Enchiladas Sonora style

This is a variation on Enchiladas Coloradas, typical in the state of Sonora, Mexico, and a favorite style served in New Mexico.

1. Prepare the sauce, filling, tortillas, and garnish ingredients as for Enchiladas Coloradas (see page 64). Enchiladas Sonora may also be garnished with a fried egg.

2. Preheat oven to 350° F. After coating the tortillas with the enchilada sauce, instead of filling and rolling, place a tortilla flat in a baking dish. Place a layer of filling over the entire tortilla, sprinkle with cheese, and top with another tortilla. Repeat this process until you have a stack of enchiladas. These can be stacked high and cut into wedges to serve or may be a small stack for an individual serving.

3. Bake until the cheese is melted. Garnish as for Enchiladas Coloradas or top with a fried egg.

Makes 1 dozen enchiladas.

Enchiladas Coloradas is a hearty, flavorful dish, perfect for an informal dinner party. For a family supper, enchiladas are a nice change of pace from the more common casseroles. In addition, they can be made ahead and then reheated to serve.

ENCHILADAS VERDES
Green enchiladas

This recipe features an excellent green sauce for enchiladas that is an elegant variation quite different from the usual enchilada sauces. The distinctive flavors of the chiles, tomatillos, and cilantro blend to create a unique and fresh-tasting sauce. Unusual in this recipe is the use of romaine lettuce, which thickens the sauce and also provides an additional dimension to the flavor.

Sauce

- 6 poblano chiles, roasted, peeled, seeded, and chopped (if unavailable, use 6 mild green chiles, roasted, peeled, seeded, and chopped and *half a bell pepper, seeded and chopped. This combination will approach the taste of the poblano chile)*
- 2 cans (12 oz each) tomatillos, drained
  Half an onion, chopped
- 2 cloves garlic, chopped
- 3 leaves romaine lettuce, torn
- ¼ cup chopped cilantro
- 1½ teaspoons salt
- 1½ cups chicken broth
- 2 tablespoons oil

Filling

Have prepared one recipe of any of the following fillings:

- *Puerco (see page 76)*
- *Pollo (see page 77)*
- *Pescado (see page 77)*
- *Queso (1½ lbs grated cheese)*
- *Queso Blanco (see page 77)*

To Assemble

- 1 dozen corn tortillas
  Oil ¼ inch deep, for frying
- ¼ pound cheese (jack, feta, or farmer or Mexican queso fresco), grated or crumbled
  Garnishes: Sour cream, radish rosettes, avocado slices, and whole ripe olives

1. *To prepare the sauce:* Place chiles, tomatillos, onion, garlic, lettuce, cilantro, salt, and ½ cup of the chicken broth in a blender or food processor. Blend to a smooth purée.

2. In a skillet heat 2 tablespoons oil, add purée, and cook over medium heat for 3 minutes, stirring constantly. Slowly stir in the remaining chicken broth and cook until sauce thickens (5 to 10 minutes longer). Keep warm.

3. *To assemble the enchiladas:* Preheat oven to 350° F. Heat oil in a skillet over high heat to 400° to 425° F. (Oil is sufficiently hot when a tiny bit of tortilla dropped into it pops immediately to the surface.) Fry each tortilla, one at a time, only long enough to soften it (a few seconds per side). Lift the tortilla with tongs and move it into the warm sauce. Turn to coat well on both sides, then lift to a plate. Place some of the prepared filling across the middle of the tortilla, fold, and place seam side down in a baking pan. Repeat this process with each tortilla.

4. Spoon a small amount of the remaining sauce across each enchilada, paying particular attention to coating the ends. Sprinkle the grated cheese over the enchiladas, cover the pan tightly with foil, and bake until heated through (20 to 30 minutes).

5. Garnish enchiladas before serving.

Makes 1 dozen enchiladas.

ENCHILADAS DE MOLE
Enchiladas in mole poblano

These enchiladas use the classic cooking sauce of Mexico, mole poblano. This sauce is traditionally used for the Christmas turkey and other special occasions throughout the year. Except at Christmas, it is usually served with chicken. These enchiladas are the happy result of "leftovers" from the Christmas feast. This sauce, however, is the most commonly used sauce for enchiladas in the southern part of Mexico.

- *Mole Poblano, the sauce only (see page 90)*
- *Pollo con Mole (see page 77)*
- 1 dozen corn tortillas
  Oil ¼ inch deep, for frying
- ¼ pound jack cheese, grated
  Garnishes: sour cream, fresh cilantro, whole ripe olives, and toasted sesame seeds

1. Prepare the mole poblano sauce and the filling according to directions. Keep warm in a large saucepan over a burner on low heat.

2. Preheat oven to 350° F. Heat oil in a skillet over high heat to 400° to 425° F. (Oil is sufficiently hot when a tiny bit of tortilla dropped into it pops immediately to the surface.) Fry each tortilla, one at a time, only long enough to soften it (a few seconds per side). Lift the tortilla with tongs and move it into the prepared mole sauce. Turn to coat well on both sides; then place on a plate. Put some of the prepared filling across the middle of the tortilla, roll, and place seam side down in a baking pan. Repeat this process with each tortilla.

3. Spoon a small amount of the remaining sauce across each enchilada, paying particular attention to coating the ends. Sprinkle grated cheese over the enchiladas, cover the pan tightly with foil, and bake until heated thoroughly and cheese is melted (20 to 30 minutes).

4. Garnish enchiladas with cilantro, olives, sour cream, or sesame seed. Serve warm.

Makes 1 dozen enchiladas.

ENCHILADAS DE MOLE II
Enchiladas in mole poblano

This is a simplified version of the classic enchiladas de mole. It requires a jar of prepared mole poblano, which is sold in ethnic shopping areas in the United States. Use this recipe as a convenient timesaver for the sauce portion of Enchiladas de Mole, then proceed with the ingredients and instructions in the main recipe (see opposite page).

    1 *jar (8 oz) prepared mole*
        poblano paste
    3½ *cups chicken broth*

1. Pour into a skillet the oil that has separated to the top of the jar of mole paste. Heat oil over medium heat, add paste, and briefly fry for 3 minutes. Slowly add the chicken broth, stirring constantly. Bring to a boil, reduce heat, and simmer 5 minutes. Keep warm.

2. See Enchiladas de Mole, page 66. Prepare filling and proceed with the instructions for assembling and serving the enchiladas (steps 2 through 4).

ENCHILADAS SUIZAS
Swiss-style enchiladas

This Swiss-style enchilada is served in some restaurants throughout Mexico. It is called Swiss-style because it includes whipping cream, a common ingredient in Switzerland, but one not typical to Mexican cooking. This recipe is a variation of Enchiladas Verdes.

1. Prepare the sauce and fill the tortillas as for Enchiladas Verdes (see page 66). After preparing the enchiladas and placing them in the baking dish, cover them evenly with 1 cup whipping cream. Preheat oven to 350° F. Bake, uncovered, for 15 to 20 minutes.

2. Garnish with avocado slices and radish rosettes before serving.

Enchiladas may be stacked or rolled or folded, as long as they are "chilied"—the variations in fillings, sauces, and garnishes offer endless possibilities. Here you see Enchiladas Verdes, or green enchiladas, and Enchiladas de Mole—enchiladas in a mole poblano sauce.

Sopes can be filled and garnished in a multitude of ways. These sopes are filled with shredded chicken and then topped with crumbled cheese, lettuce, cilantro, and red onion. A green salsa completes the picture.

THICK MASA DISHES

Sopes, gordas, tamales, and other Mexican dishes can be designated thick masa creations. That is, they don't use thin tortillas but rather are made from fresh masa dough.

Sopes are circular pieces of dough with raised edges that hold a variety of fillings, such as a layer of beans, shredded meat, and salsa and fresh garnishes. Sopes are also known as gordas in some regions. Gordas may also refer to little, fat tortillas, sometimes made with the addition of thick cream or mashed potatoes mixed into the masa. When this type of gorda is made in a shape like a flat football it becomes a memelo, and if it has a filling it is known as clacollo. If the sope is elongated it is called a chalupa, referring to its

canoe shape. With the exception of the tamale, most of these masa creations are first cooked on the comal and then fried just before being filled and served.

SOPES

The masa shells for the sopes may be made in advance and frozen uncooked. Completely thaw the frozen shells before frying and assembling.

Shells

¼ cup shortening
2 cups masa harina or 1 pound fresh masa dough
1¼ cups warm water (omit if using fresh masa)
   Oil ¼ inch deep, for frying
   Salt

Filling

   Frijoles Refritos (see page 53; optional)
   Carnitas (see page 86) or Pollo (see page 77)

Garnishes

   Salsa Verde (see page 22) or Salsa de Chipotle (see page 22)
   Shredded iceberg lettuce
   Radishes, chopped
   Green onion, sliced
   Cebolla en Lima (see page 25)
   Fresh cilantro
   Crumbled queso fresco or feta cheese that has been rinsed and patted dry

1. To prepare the shells: Preheat oven to 425° F. In a large mixing bowl, cream shortening; add masa harina alternately with water, mixing well after each addition. (If using fresh masa, omit the water and mix small amounts at a time into the shortening.) Divide the dough into 8 equal pieces. Shape each ball into a flat circle approximately ⅛ inch thick. Pinch up the edge to make a ¼-inch rim.

2. Place on a baking sheet and bake for 12 to 15 minutes. Set aside and allow to cool while preparing the fillings and garnishes.

3. *To assemble sopes:* Heat oil in a skillet over high heat to 425° F. Lightly salt the sope shells and fry a few at a time, spooning oil into the center, and turning over once. Cook until golden (about 4 minutes). Drain on paper towels.

4. Fill the sopes by spreading a thin layer of Frijoles Refritos (if used) into the bottom. Add some of the Carnitas or Pollo Filling.

5. Garnish the sopes before serving.

Makes 8 sopes.

SOPITOS DE COLIMA
Little sopes

> *Masa for sopito shells
> (see Sope Shell recipe
> opposite page)
> Shredded Meat Filling
> (see page 73)
> Grated Parmesan or
> Romano cheese
> Sliced onions, shredded
> lettuce, and radishes, for
> garnish*

1. Form small olive-sized balls of masa. Press them out, either by hand or in a tortilla press, into thin 2-inch circles.

2. Cook the rounds on a very lightly greased griddle or comal. When firm enough to handle, remove from the griddle and allow to cool slightly. Form a lip or raised edge around each and set aside until ready to assemble.

3. *To assemble sopitos:* Heat oil to 425° F. Deep-fry sopito shells in hot oil until crisp and golden (about 3 minutes). Drain on paper towels.

4. Put a spoonful of the meat filling into each shell. Top with grated Parmesan and garnish with sliced onion, shredded lettuce, and sliced radishes. Serve at once.

Serves 4 to 6.

PANUCHOS
Corn tortilla pockets

Panuchos, typical to the more southern regions of Mexico, make an excellent party food or a delicious and unusual family meal.

> *Frijoles Refritos (see page 53)
> Hard-boiled eggs
> Pollo Filling (page 77)
> Oil ¼ inch deep, for frying
> Garnishes: Sour cream, avocado, salsa, Cebolla en Lima
> (see page 25), cilantro, and
> crumbled queso fresco*

1. Prepare masa as for Tortillas de Maiz (see page 56). Divide dough into 12 balls.

2. Shape each ball into a small, thick tortilla. Cook as for tortillas but for a slightly longer time because of the thicker dough. When the tortilla puffs during the cooking, cut a "pocket" near the edge and follow around one fourth of the tortilla edge.

3. Spread a layer of the prepared Frijoles Refritos inside each panucho "pocket." Top the beans with a slice of egg. Press the edges together to seal the filling inside the pocket.

4. Heat oil over medium-high heat to 400° to 425° F. Lightly salt the panuchos and fry a few at a time (bean side down), occasionally basting the top with the hot oil. Fry until the underside is slightly crisp. Drain on paper towels.

5. To serve, place a small amount of Pollo Filling on the panucho and top with the garnishes.

Makes 1 dozen panuchos.

HOW TO MAKE SOPES

Sopes are easy to make when you follow the steps given here.

1. *Moisten hands with water and form masa into walnut-size balls. Pat balls into cakes about 3 inches across and ¼ inch thick.*

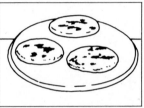

2. *Partially cook the cakes on a dry comal to set the masa.*

3. *Pinch up the edges of the partially baked masa to form rim of sopa about ⅝ inch high. This will hold the filling.*

4. *Fry sopes one at a time in hot oil until golden brown. Spoon hot fat into centers to cook top surface of sopes.*

Fresh tamales have a flavor and richness all their own. The corn-husk wrapping enhances the corn flavor and keeps the masa moist. Tamales can be filled with a variety of both savory and sweet fillings.

TAMALES

Tamales are made throughout Mexico. Thick masa spread on dried corn husks and wrapped around a variety of fillings makes a *tamal*. In the tropical Gulf Coast and around Oaxaca, tamales are wrapped not in corn husks but in banana leaves, which impart a distinctive flavor. Many Americans, even in the Southwest, where Mexican foods are most popular, are familiar only with the "hot tamale" of the restaurant combination plate or the frozen foods section of their local market. This chile-and-meat-stuffed tamal is but one of an infinite variety, and the American version, usually made with too much masa and covered with a sauce, is not typical to Mexico.

In Mexico tamales can be filled with pork, beef, cracklings, venison or other game, poultry, seafood, beans or beans and chile, fresh corn and chile, cheese and chile, and many other combinations. There is the small, sweet tamalito, too heavy to be a dessert but delicious as a snack or for breakfast. Tamalitos may be filled with fruit, berries, nuts, raisins, or even beans, sweetened and spiced with cinnamon and cloves.

There are even tamales with no filling at all. One example is the Tamales Blancos (see page 72), which are traditionally served at Christmas to accompany the main dish, mole poblano. Another favorite tamale is the *tamale de elote* (fresh corn tamale). This tamale is made from a slightly sweetened dough of fresh corn that is wrapped in fresh corn husks (not dried ones) and steamed. Tamales de elote are popular for breakfast or snacks and sometimes appear on menus in restaurants or hotels. Usually, however, they are purchased in quantity to take home from tamale de elote stands. These stands are a common sight along roads and highways near towns. Unfortunately, the corn grown in the United States is too "juicy" for tamales de elote and therefore you cannot duplicate this recipe here.

Tamales are party and fiesta fare for birthdays, christenings, weddings, All Saint's Day, and, especially, for New Year's. The old saying "too many cooks . . ." doesn't apply to a *tamalada*, a tamale-making get-together; there are plenty of jobs to go around for family and friends of all ages.

Specially designed tamale steamers are available; however, a vegetable steamer or canning kettle will work. It is important to set the tamales above the boiling water during the cooking process. You may adapt any large pot (with a lid) to suit this need by placing small empty cans in the bottom and adding water not quite to the top of the cans.

TAMALES

Although a wide variety of fillings may be used, a pork filling is the most traditional. This recipe will yield a dozen tamales, but you can double it in order to fill the steamer. Extra tamales can be frozen; thaw them thoroughly before reheating.

- ½ pound dried corn husks
- 2 pounds boneless pork butt or shoulder, cut into 1-inch cubes
- 4 dried ancho chiles
- 2 dried California chiles (you may substitute 6 table-spoons ground mild red chile, unseasoned, for the ancho and California chiles)
- 2 tablespoons lard or oil
  Half an onion, chopped
- 2 cloves garlic, minced
- ½ teaspoon dried oregano
- ¼ teaspoon ground cumin
- ⅛ teaspoon ground cloves
- ½ teaspoon salt or to taste
- 1 cup reserved pork broth
- ⅓ cup lard or shortening
- 2 cups masa harina or 1 pound fresh masa dough
- ½ teaspoon salt
- 1½ cups reserved pork broth (reduce this amount if using fresh masa)
- 1 tablespoon sauce from the prepared pork filling (optional)

1. Soak the corn husks in hot water, removing any corn silk. Open the husks flat and stand them to drain until needed, but do not allow them to dry hard before being used. The husks should be soft but not wet when you assemble the tamales.

2. *To prepare the filling:* Cover the meat with water and simmer until almost tender, 40 minutes. Drain meat, reserving the broth. Coarsely chop the meat.

3. Remove and discard the seeds and stems from the chiles. Place chiles on a preheated heavy frying pan or comal. Over medium heat lightly toast the chiles, turning frequently. Allow to cool. Crumble the chiles into a blender and grind to a fine powder.

4. Heat the 2 tablespoons lard in a large skillet and sauté onion and garlic, cooking only until soft. Add oregano, cumin, cloves, and ground chile; stir and cook briefly. Stir in meat and salt and cook briefly. Slowly stir in 1 cup of the pork broth and cook 5 minutes over medium heat. Set aside to cool while preparing the dough.

5. *To prepare the dough:* In a large bowl, beat the ⅓ cup lard until fluffy. Mix together masa harina and salt. Alternately add small amounts of the masa harina and broth into the lard, mixing well after each addition. (If using fresh masa dough rather than masa harina, add it to the lard in small amounts, alternately with small amounts of the broth, beating well after each addition.) The dough is the desired consistency if it is just dry enough to hold together yet moist enough to spread easily. Mix in 1 tablespoon of the sauce from the filling mixture, if desired.

6. *To assemble tamales:* Place water in the bottom of the steamer. The tamales must set above the water during the entire cooking process (see directions, page 72). Line the steamer with a double layer of corn husks across the bottom rack and up the sides.

7. Hold a prepared corn husk in the palm of the hand; spread approximately 2 tablespoons masa in a thin square-shaped layer in the center of each husk. Place a large spoonful of the filling in the middle of the dough.

Roll the husk around the filling, making sure both ends of the masa join together, and turn the ends of the husk down. Wrap in an additional husk and tie with strips torn from husks or with string. The idea is to make a little waterproof package for the tamale to cook in.

8. Stand the tamales upright in the steamer as they are made. Do not pack them too tight. If you do not have enough tamales to keep them standing upright during cooking, fill in the empty spaces with extra corn husks. Spread another layer of corn husks across the top of the packed tamales. Place the lid on the steamer.

9. Bring to a boil over high heat. Reduce to medium and steam for 2½ hours. It may be necessary to add water during the cooking process. If so, add hot water by carefully pulling the husks away from the side of the pot and slowly pouring the hot water down the side. The tamales are done when the masa falls cleanly away from the husk. Should the masa still be sticking to the husk, allow the tamales to steam for an additional 20 to 30 minutes.

Makes 1 dozen tamales.

Oven Method Wrap the tamales in foil and heat in a 350° F oven for 20 to 30 minutes.

Note To reheat, place the tamales on an ungreased heavy frying pan or comal over medium heat, turning occasionally until the husks are browned and the tamale is heated through (about 10 minutes).

HOW TO MAKE TAMALES

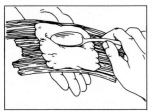

1. *Once corn husks are steamed and softened, take the broadest husks in the palm of the hand. Using the back of a tablespoon, spread a thin layer of masa in the center of each husk. Then put a spoonful of the meat mixture in the middle of the masa square.*

2. *Roll the husk around the masa and meat filling without squeezing.*

3. *Wrap with a second husk that has also been spread with masa. Tie both ends with strips of husks or string.*

4. *Place finished tamales in a steamer, standing on end. Steam for 1 hour.*

TAMALES BLANCOS
Unfilled tamales

This tamale takes its place of honor as an accompaniment to the mole poblano served for holidays and festive occasions (see page 90). This is a small, plain, unfilled tamale with a simple taste. Tamales blancos freeze well; thaw them thoroughly before reheating

> ½ pound dried corn husks
> ½ cup lard or shortening
> 2 cups masa harina or 1 pound fresh masa dough
> ½ teaspoon salt
> 1½ teaspoons baking powder
> 1½ cups warmed chicken broth (reduce this amount if using fresh masa)

1. Soak the corn husks in hot water, removing any corn silk. Open the husks flat and stand them to drain until needed, but do not allow them to dry hard before being used. The husks should be soft but not wet when you assemble the tamales.

2. In a large bowl beat the lard until fluffy. Mix together the masa harina, salt, and baking powder. Gradually beat the dry ingredients and broth alternately into the lard. (If using fresh masa dough rather than masa harina, add it to the lard in small amounts alternately with small amounts of broth, beating well after each addition.) The dough is the desired consistency if it is dry enough to hold together yet moist enough to spread easily.

3. *To assemble:* Place water in the bottom of the steamer. The tamales must set above the water during the entire cooking process (see directions at left). Line the steamer with a double layer of corn husks across the bottom rack and up the sides.

4. Hold a prepared corn husk in the palm of the hand, spread approximately 2 tablespoons masa in the center of each husk. Roll the husk and turn the ends of the husk down. Wrap in an additional husk if necessary and tie with strips torn from husks or with string. The idea is to make a little waterproof package for the tamale to cook in.

5. Pack the tamales upright in the steamer. Do not pack them too tight. If you do not have enough tamales to keep them standing upright during cooking, fill in the empty spaces with extra corn husks. Spread another layer of corn husks across the top of the packed tamales. Place the lid on the steamer.

6. Bring to a boil over high heat. Reduce to medium and steam for 1½ hours. It may be necessary to add water during the cooking process; if so, add hot water by carefully pulling the husks away from the side of the pot and slowly pouring the water down the side of the pot. The tamale is done when it falls cleanly away from the husk. Should the masa still be sticking to the husk, allow the tamales to steam for an additional 20 to 30 minutes.

Makes 1 dozen tamales.

Oven Method Wrap the tamales in foil and heat in a 350° F oven for 20 to 30 minutes.

Note To reheat, place the tamales on an ungreased heavy frying pan or comal over medium heat; turn occasionally until the husks are browned and the tamale heated through (about 10 minutes).

THE FILLINGS

In Mexico the fillings used for the masa dishes are usually shredded meats that are succulent, juicy, and full flavored. Seldom is ground meat used in Mexican cuisine. The ground beef fillings so often served in the United States are not authentic and don't compare in flavor or texture with shredded meat. The use of ground meat is a convenient timesaver, however.

There is a secret to the preparation of the succulent shredded meats. The meat is first covered with cold water and simmered until tender. Salt or other seasonings are not added during this initial cooking process because they would draw the flavor and juices out of the meat and into the broth. (This is desirable if you're making a soup or stew but not when the objective is to retain the full flavor and juiciness of the meat.) The meat is then cooled in its own broth before being removed and shredded. These two steps are important keys to authentic shredded meats.

In addition to the recipes featured here, there are many recipes elsewhere in the book that can be used for fillings. For beef fillings, try Carne Asada (see page 80), Chile Colorado (see page 81), or Machaca (see page 84). For pork fillings, try Carnitas (see page 86), Chile Verde (see page 86), or Chorizo (see page 88). Birria (see page 89) would make an excellent lamb filling, and Huachinango a la Veracruzana (see page 96) could be used as a fish filling. Use as fillings for tacos, flautas, burritos, chimichangas, tortas, empanadas, or sopes. Another good filling for tacos, burritos, or chimichangas is Huevos con Nopales (see page 108).

The following recipe is the basic, simple method for making shredded meat filling using either beef, pork, or chicken. Use this recipe to initiate yourself to shredded meat cookery, Mexican style. You will soon want to try the other filling recipes.

BASIC SHREDDED MEAT RECIPE

This filling may be used to fill tacos, enchiladas, flautas, burritos, chimichangas, and sopes or to top panuchos or tostadas.

Use one of the following meats:

> *Beef: chuck roast, cut into 2-inch cubes*
> *Pork: boneless butt or shoulder, cut into 1-inch cubes*
> *Chicken: a whole chicken, cut into pieces (for special dishes use boned chicken breasts)*
> *Salt*
> *Oregano*
> *Cumin (for beef)*
> *Half an onion, chopped (optional)*
> 1 *clove garlic, minced (optional)*
> 1 *tablespoon lard or oil (optional)*

1. Place the meat in a pot and cover with cold water. Bring to a boil, cover, and simmer. For beef, simmer 1½ hours or until tender; for pork, simmer 40 minutes or until tender; for chicken, simmer pieces 35 minutes or until cooked. Poach boned chicken breasts 15 minutes or until cooked.

2. Allow meat to cool in broth until easy to handle.

3. Remove the meat and discard any fatty pieces; for chicken, discard the skin and bones. The meat may be shredded by using your fingers or two forks; however, it is more easily shredded in a food processor using the plastic blade: Place a few pieces of meat at a time into the container and process briefly (do not shred the meat too fine).

4. After shredding the meat, add salt to taste and a dash of oregano (for beef, also add a dash of cumin). Mix together.

5. Sauté onion and garlic (if used) in the lard in a skillet; cook until soft. Add the shredded meat and cook, stirring, until heated through.

CHORIZO Y PAPAS
Sausage and potato filling

Chorizo is the sausage of Mexico. Its spicy, hearty taste is unique and unmistakable. A good-quality chorizo is not always available in markets here but making your own is easy (see page 88), and worth the effort. Use this recipe as a main dish accompanied by warm tortillas or as a filling for tacos, burritos, chimichangas, tortas, empanadas, enchiladas coloradas, or sopes.

> 1 *pound chorizo*
> 1 *clove garlic, minced*
> *Half an onion, chopped*
> 2 *medium potatoes, cooked, peeled, and diced*
> 1 *tomato, chopped*
> *Chopped cilantro leaves (optional)*

1. Peel the chorizo and crumble into a skillet. Sauté until browned, about 20 minutes. Add garlic and onion and cook until soft.

2. Stir in potatoes and tomato. Cook, stirring occasionally, until the potatoes are heated through (about 15 minutes). Stir in cilantro (if used).

Serves 3 to 4 as a main dish.

Picadillo de Res is a wonderful beef filling that includes apples, raisins, cinnamon, and cloves. It has a sweet spiciness that's simply irresistible.

ROPA VIEJA
Old clothes

In spite of its unusual name, variations of ropa vieja are common in most Mexican households. This recipe is similar to many served under the more appealing name of machaca in restaurants in the southwestern United States. It is made with a shredded beef called cecina. (See explanation of traditional machaca, page 84.) This filling is most commonly used for burritos; however, it may also be used for tacos, flautas, chimichangas, tortas, and empanadas or it may be served as a main dish accompanied by warm tortillas.

  1 pound chuck roast, cut into
    2-inch cubes
    Half an onion, chopped
  1 clove garlic, minced
  2 tablespoons lard or oil
  3 tomatoes, chopped
  2 jalapeño chiles, chopped
    or 1 can (4 oz) diced green
    chiles for a milder taste
    Salt to taste
  3 eggs, beaten

1. Place meat in a pot and cover with cold water. Bring to a boil, cover, and simmer until tender, 1 to 1½ hours. Allow the meat to cool in the broth until easy to handle.

2. Remove the meat and shred by using your fingers or two forks. The meat will also shred easily in a food processor using the plastic blade: Place a few pieces at a time into the container and process briefly (avoid shredding the meat too fine).

3. Sauté onion and garlic in the lard until the onion is soft. Add tomatoes and chiles and cook until the tomatoes are soft. Mix in the meat, check the seasoning, and salt to taste.

4. Lower the heat and add the beaten eggs. Stir to keep the egg from forming an omelet and cook until the eggs are set. May be served as a main dish or as a filling.

Serves 4 as a main dish.

RES
Beef filling

This is one of the most common shredded meat fillings served in Mexico. Use this filling for tacos, flautas, burritos, chimichangas, tortas, empanadas, enchiladas coloradas, and sopes.

  3 pounds chuck roast, cut
    into 2-inch cubes
  3 tablespoons lard or oil
  1 onion, chopped
  2 cloves garlic, minced
  2 teaspoons dried oregano
  1 teaspoon ground cumin
  1 teaspoon salt
  1 can (16 oz) solid-pack
    tomatoes, puréed in blender

1. Place meat in a pot and cover with cold water. Bring to a boil, cover, and simmer 1½ hours. Allow meat to cool in the broth until easy to handle.

2. Remove meat and shred by using fingers or two forks. The meat will also shred easily in a food processor using the plastic blade: Place a few pieces of meat at a time into the container and process briefly (avoid shredding the meat too fine).

3. Heat lard in a large skillet, add shredded meat, and cook until lightly browned. Add onion and garlic and cook until the onion is soft. Stir in oregano, cumin, and salt. Slowly add the tomato purée and simmer, uncovered, for 30 minutes, stirring occasionally until done. If necessary, add small amounts of beef broth or water to maintain a moist mixture.

Makes enough filling for 10 tacos, burritos, flautas, or enchiladas.

PICADILLO DE RES
Spiced beef filling

Picadillo is a spiced meat filling with fruit added to the mixture. It's a refreshing combination of the sweet and the savory. In Mexico it is used as a filling for special-occasion masa dishes. Use it to fill Chiles Rellenos (see page 48), Chiles en Nogada (see page 48), Empanadas (see page 60), and Sopes (see page 68). It is also good just wrapped in warm tortillas.

  1 pound lean beef, coarsely
    chopped or cooked and
    shredded
  2 tablespoons lard or oil
  1 onion, diced
  1 clove garlic, minced
  2 tomatoes, chopped
  1 apple, peeled, cored, and
    chopped
  ¼ cup seedless raisins, plumped
    in hot water and drained
  ⅛ teaspoon ground cinnamon
    Pinch each ground cloves and
    ground cumin
  ½ cup broth or water
    Salt to taste

1. Sauté meat in the oil or lard until browned. Add onion and garlic and cook until soft.

2. Add tomatoes, apple, raisins, cinnamon, cloves, cumin, and broth. Simmer until liquid is absorbed (about 25 minutes). Check the seasoning and salt to taste.

Makes enough filling for 8 to 10 empanadas.

PUERCO
Pork filling

Ground meat is seldom used in Mexican cuisine; however, this recipe using ground pork provides a simple and quick filling with good texture and authentic flavor. This filling, especially good for sopes, can be used also for tacos, flautas, burritos, chimichangas, and empanadas.

    1 dried ancho chile
    ½ cup boiling water
    1 tomato, chopped
    1 pound ground pork
    1 onion, chopped
    1 clove garlic, minced
    1 can (4 oz) diced green chiles
      or 1 jalapeño, chopped, for a
      hotter dish
    ½ teaspoon dried oregano
    ¼ teaspoon ground cumin
      Salt to taste
    1 potato, cooked, peeled,
      and diced

1. Remove seeds and veins from the ancho chile. Wash ancho and soak in the boiling water for 30 minutes. Place the ancho, water, and tomato into a blender or food processor and purée until smooth.

2. Crumble pork into a skillet and cook until browned (about 20 minutes) over medium high heat.
Add onion and garlic and cook until soft. Add the diced green chiles, oregano, and cumin. Stir in the ancho-tomato purée, check the seasoning, and salt to taste.

3. Add potato and heat, stirring occasionally, until the potato is heated through.

Makes enough filling for 8 to 10 sopes.

PICADILLO DE PUERCO
Spiced pork filling

Picadillo is a spiced meat filling with fruit added to the mixture. As with Picadillo de Res (see page 75), it is used as a filling for special-occasion masa dishes. Use to fill Chiles Rellenos (see page 48), Chiles en Nogada (see page 48), Empanadas (see page 60), and Sopes (see page 68).

    1 pound lean pork, coarsely
      chopped
    1 tablespoon lard or oil
    1 onion, diced
    1 clove garlic, minced
    1 tomato, chopped
    ½ cup olives
    1 apple, peeled, cored,
      and chopped
    ¼ cup almonds, chopped
    ¼ cup seedless raisins, plumped
      in hot water and drained
    ⅛ teaspoon ground cinnamon
      Pinch ground cloves
      Salt to taste

1. Place meat in a skillet and add boiling water to barely cover. Cover and cook until tender; then uncover and cook over medium heat until the liquid has evaporated.

2. Add lard and sauté onion and garlic until soft. Add tomato, olives, apple, almonds, raisins, cinnamon, and cloves and cook, stirring, for 5 to 6 minutes. Check the seasoning and salt to taste.

Makes enough filling for 6 to 8 Chiles en Nogada.

POLLO CON TOMATILLOS
Chicken filling with tomatillos

Shredded chicken is an excellent filling for masa dishes and this recipe, using the unique flavor of tomatillos, makes a tasty filling. Use as a filling for tacos, flautas, burritos, chimichangas, tortas, empanadas, enchiladas verdes, enchiladas Suizas, and sopes, and as a topping for panuchos and tostadas.

    1 whole chicken, cut into pieces
    1 onion, chopped
    2 cloves garlic, minced
    2 tablespoons oil
    1 can (12 oz) tomatillos,
      drained and mashed
    ½ teaspoon salt
    ¼ cup cilantro leaves, coarsely
      chopped

1. Cover the chicken with cold water, bring to a boil, cover, reduce heat, and simmer for 35 minutes or until tender. Allow the chicken to cool in the broth until easy to handle.

2. Remove the chicken and discard the skin and bones. Shred by using your fingers or two forks. The chicken will also shred easily in a food processor using the plastic blade: Place a few pieces at a time into the container and process briefly (avoid shredding too fine).

3. In a skillet sauté onion and garlic in the oil and cook until soft. Add tomatillos and salt. Bring to a boil, reduce heat, and cook 5 minutes to reduce the liquid. Add chicken and cilantro and cook for 10 minutes.

Makes enough filling for 12 tacos, flautas, empanadas, chimichangas, or enchiladas or 8 burritos.

POLLO CON MOLE
Chicken filling with mole

Use this filling for Enchiladas de Mole (see page 66). Any leftover cooked chicken or turkey can be used.

  1 whole chicken, cut into pieces
  1 onion, chopped
  2 cloves garlic, minced
  2 tablespoons oil
  ¾ cup sauce from Mole Poblano (see page 90)
  Salt to taste

1. Cover chicken with cold water, bring to a boil, cover, and simmer over low heat for 35 minutes or until tender. Allow chicken to cool in the broth until easy to handle.

2. Remove chicken and discard the skin and bones. Cut into small pieces.

3. In a skillet, sauté onion and garlic in the oil and cook until soft. Add the chicken pieces and the sauce. Check the seasoning and salt to taste. Reduce heat and simmer until the chicken is heated through.

Makes enough filling for 12 tacos, flautas, empanadas, chimichangas, or enchiladas or 8 burritos.

POLLO
Chicken filling

  3 boned chicken breasts, poached
  Salt
  Dash of oregano

1. Poach the chicken breasts in the broth and allow to cool in the broth.

2. Remove skin and discard. Shred by using fingers or two forks. The meat will also shred easily in a food processor using the plastic blade: Cut chicken into chunks, place a few pieces at a time into the container, and process briefly.

3. Lightly salt the chicken and sprinkle with oregano; mix together.

Makes enough filling for 12 tacos, flautas, empanadas, chimichangas, or enchiladas or 8 burritos.

CAMARON
Shrimp filling

This elegant filling is used to top tostadas and to fill flautas, tacos, tortas, empanadas, and, especially, taquitos, the miniature tacos.

  2 tablespoons butter
  Half an onion, diced
  1½ pounds shrimp, chopped
  3 fresh poblano chiles, roasted, peeled, seeded, and chopped or 1 can (4 oz) diced green chiles

In a skillet, melt butter and sauté onion until soft. Add shrimp and chiles. Cook, stirring, to heat through.

Makes enough filling for 8 empanadas or tacos.

PESCADO
Fish filling

Although pescado is used extensively as a filling for masa dishes in Mexico, it is rarely served in the United States. Use it to fill tacos, flautas, burritos, chimichangas, tortas, empanadas, enchiladas, and sopes.

  2 pounds red snapper fillets, cut into bite-sized pieces (any fish with a similar texture may be used)
  ¼ cup olive oil
  1 onion, chopped
  2 cloves garlic, minced
  3 tomatoes, chopped
  3 fresh poblano chiles, roasted, peeled, seeded, and chopped or 1 can (7 oz) whole green chiles, rinsed and chopped
  Salt to taste

1. In a skillet sauté the fish in olive oil until tender and easily flaked with a fork. Add onion and garlic and cook until soft.

2. Add tomatoes and chiles and cook until soft. Check the seasoning and salt to taste, if necessary.

Makes enough filling for 12 tacos or enchiladas or 8 empanadas or burritos.

CHEESE FILLINGS

The white cheeses used in Mexico are not always available in the United States. Jack, Colby, mild Cheddar, or similar cheeses will work just as well.

QUESO Y CEBOLLA
Cheese and onion filling

  1 pound Colby, jack, or mild Cheddar cheese, grated
  2 cans (2¼ oz each) sliced ripe olives
  1 onion, chopped

1. Set aside 1 cup of the grated cheese.

2. Mix together olives and onion. Fill each enchilada by placing a handful of cheese in the center of the prepared tortilla. Top with a spoonful of the onion and olive mixture. Roll and proceed with the enchilada recipe of your choice.

3. Top the finished enchiladas with the 1 cup grated cheese and bake according to the recipe.

Makes enough filling for 1 dozen enchiladas.

QUESO BLANCO
White cheese filling

This is a creamy cheese filling that doesn't really melt. It is a substitute for a similar cheese used in Mexico. The texture is smooth and delightful.

  1 pound ricotta cheese
  ¼ pound feta cheese, rinsed and patted dry, and crumbled

1. Mix the cheeses together until creamy.

2. Fill each enchilada by placing a handful of the cheese mixture in the center of the prepared tortilla. Roll and proceed with the enchilada recipe of your choice.

Makes 2½ cups.

Mexican cuisine employs ingenious methods to bring out the distinctive flavors and unusual textures in meat, fish, shellfish, and poultry.

Meat, Poultry & Seafood

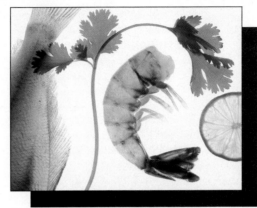

Meat, poultry, and seafood play special roles in Mexican cuisine. This chapter features traditional recipes and methods of preparation so that the special flavors of Mexican cooking can come to life in your kitchen. You will find recipes for everything from steak to seviche. For a change of pace, instead of an ordinary dinner party carry out a Mexican theme with flair and sophistication by preparing one of the fine recipes featured in this chapter. Your guests will be delighted with the change.

MEXICAN MEAT

In Mexico, as elsewhere, the tenderest cuts of meat are usually grilled in the most straightforward manner, but great ingenuity is displayed in the preparation of those less tender and often more flavorful cuts of meat. Meat cutters in Mexico traditionally slice with the grain (steak cut across the grain is a recent innovation), and this "with the grain" method of cutting meat is entirely logical, considering how meat is preserved and prepared for the table. Meat is generally bought in small quantities in Mexico because it is used in many Mexican dishes as a savory addition, much as it is used in Chinese cooking. If the meat is to be shredded, it is easier to shred when the grain runs the length rather than the depth of the cut.

In the United States the "innards" of an animal are often discarded—the by-product of abundance coupled with a surfeit of delicacy. In Mexico, as in many other cultures, none of the animal is wasted. Clearly our sensibilities do us no credit in this matter; the spectrum of choices is restricted and nourishment curtailed.

BEEF

Traditional Mexican methods of cooking beef are often designed for a cut of meat from an animal that has done a bit of walking around. Steak as served in the United States is not really a part of the Mexican cuisine. However, there has been a great improvement in beef quality in the last eight to ten years. This may be due to the increased use of feedlot procedures, at least for first-class restaurant meat. It may also be that government programs to introduce better breeding stock are beginning to have results in the meat market. On the other hand, pork in Mexico is tender and succulent and is often the preferred meat, particularly for stews.

Carne al pastor is certainly one of the most innovative methods for cooking meat in Mexico. Thin steaks are impaled on a spindle in a stack and then cooked vertically on an ingenious charcoal barbecue made especially for carne al pastor; it is sold from stands throughout Mexico and is a specialty in many restaurants. While this technique is far from practical for most U.S. cooks, a modified version of carne al pastor would be a great party attraction.

As the spindle is turned slowly before the fire, the cooked meat is trimmed off. Each succulent piece is like a miniature roast beef. The juicy tidbits of meat are scooped into a small tortilla, or an overlapping pair of tortillas, and the customer then adds chopped onions, tomatoes, cilantro, and a choice of salsas.

CARNE ASADA
Grilled meats

This steak is flavored with lime and garlic and then grilled. Slice thinly and place inside a warm corn or flour tortilla garnished with the salsa of your choice and grilled onions, if you like. The steaks may be fried instead of grilled, though the barbecue imparts the best flavor.

    2 to 3 pounds steak, skirt,
      rib eye, or beef tenderloin
      Juice of 4 limes
    2 cloves garlic, finely chopped
      Salt and pepper to taste
    4 tablespoons butter
    2 tablespoons oil

1. Squeeze lime juice over steaks. Rub some chopped garlic into each steak and sprinkle with salt and pepper to taste. Allow steaks to marinate for 30 minutes.

2. Prepare barbecue. Coals are sufficiently hot when you cannot hold your hand 4 inches above the coals for longer than a count of 4.

3. Melt butter in saucepan over low heat. Stir in oil. Coat each steak with this mixture. Place steaks on the barbecue and cook until done to your liking. Slice steaks with the grain and serve in a tortilla with salsa, if desired.

Serves 4 to 6.

CHILE VERDE DE RES
Green chile with beef

In Mexico chile verde is most commonly made with pork (see page 86); however, this version with beef is often served in the Mexican home. This is a flavorful and hearty stew and any leftovers will make a delicious filling for burritos. Serve accompanied by warm tortillas, a rice or bean side dish (Arroz de Mexico, page 35, or Frijoles Refritos, page 53) or Fideo (see page 36), and a green salad.

    2 pounds round steak, cut
      into 1-inch pieces
      Flour
    3 tablespoons lard or oil
    1 onion, chopped
    2 cloves garlic, minced
    5 mild green chiles, roasted,
      peeled, and cut into strips or
      1 can (7 oz) whole green
      chiles, rinsed and cut into
      strips
    1 tomato, peeled and chopped
    ½ teaspoon dried oregano
    ¼ teaspoon ground cumin
    1 cup water
      Salt to taste
      Sour cream, for garnish

1. Coat the meat with flour. Heat lard in a large skillet and brown meat.

2. Add onion and garlic and cook until soft. Add chiles, tomato, oregano, and cumin and cook 1 to 2 minutes, stirring. Slowly add the water, cover, and simmer 1 hour. Check seasoning and add salt if necessary.

3. Garnish with a dab of sour cream before serving.

Serves 6.

BISTEK RANCHERO
Ranch-style steak

This steak recipe is popular throughout Mexico as well as our own Southwest. A quick and simple recipe makes this ideal for summer entertaining and delicious for a barbecue. Serve with Frijoles Refritos (see page 53), salad, warm tortillas, and salsa.

- 2 tablespoons oil
- 1 onion, cut into thin wedges
- 2 cloves garlic, minced
- 5 mild green chiles, roasted, peeled, and cut into strips (rajas)
- 2 tomatoes, cut into thin wedges
- 2 tablespoons chopped cilantro leaves
- 2 to 3 pounds steak (choose your favorite cut), barbecued or broiled

1. Heat the oil in a skillet and sauté the onion and garlic until soft. Add chiles and tomatoes and sauté briefly until soft. Stir in cilantro and keep warm.

2. Barbecue the steaks to individual preference and serve topped with the sautéed chile-tomato mixture.

Serves 6 to 8.

CHILE COLORADO
Beef in a red chile sauce

Chile Colorado is a classic use of beef in the Mexican cuisine. Typical in northern Mexico, it is popular throughout our Southwest as well. The sauce is the cooking sauce used for the Enchiladas Coloradas. Any leftovers will make delicious burritos.

- 4 pounds chuck roast, cut into 2-inch cubes
- 1 recipe sauce from Enchiladas Coloradas (see page 64)
  Salt to taste

1. Cover the meat with cold water, bring to a boil, reduce heat, cover, and simmer until very tender (1 to 1½ hours). Allow the meat to cool in the broth until easy to handle.

2. Remove the meat and cut into bite-sized pieces. Reserve the broth.

3. Prepare salsa de chile colorado: the sauce used for Enchiladas Coloradas, (see page 64, steps 1, 2, and 3), using the reserved broth from the cooked beef instead of chicken broth. Place the beef pieces in the prepared sauce, check seasoning, and add salt if necessary. Simmer until the meat is heated through (about 15 minutes). Serve accompanied by warm tortillas.

Serves 6 to 8.

Bistek Ranchero, smothered in onions and peppers, is a great way to dress up an ordinary steak. The steak tastes best when cooked over a fire of red hot mesquite coals. Serve with rice, a green salad, and warm tortillas.

The beef in this salad is marinated in salsa and Oil and Vinegar Dressing for several hours until it acquires a spicy, tangy flavor. Serve this salad with tortillas for a summer lunch or dinner. Finish the meal with a Mexican dessert and coffee.

ENSALADA DE CARNE
Salad with marinated beef

The taco salad (seasoned ground meat added to a green salad) so popular in many parts of the United States is not typical in Mexico.

However, this recipe using marinated meat in the salad is not only authentic but delicious. If you like taco salad, be sure to try this variation. This main course salad makes a wonderful light summer meal and is a good way to use leftover beef. Serve with totopos (see page 62).

⅔ cup Oil and Vinegar Dressing (see page 44)
⅓ cup salsa (choose your favorite from the salsa recipes in this book, see page 21, or use a canned salsa)
3 cups cooked beef, cut into thin strips
1 head green leaf lettuce, torn into pieces
2 tomatoes, cut into wedges

1 cup shredded red cabbage
15 pimiento-stuffed green olives, cut in half
½ cup garbanzo beans, drained Cebolla en Lima (see page 25)
Crumbled queso fresco or feta cheese

1. In a small bowl combine dressing and salsa. Place meat in a medium bowl and pour marinade over the meat; cover and marinate in refrigerator for several hours.

2. In a large bowl mix together the lettuce, tomatoes, cabbage, olives, and garbanzos. Add the meat and dressing and toss.

3. Serve garnished with Cebolla en Lima (marinated onions) and crumbled cheese.

Serves 4 to 6.

CHILE CON CARNE Y FRIJOLES
Chili with meat and beans

Chile con carne (usually spelled "chili" in this country) is not a part of the authentic Mexican cuisine but rather falls into the category of "border foods"—those foods that have evolved along the Mexican border in the southwestern United States. Chile con carne is an excellent example of authentic Mexican ingredients used in a different way in this country. In Mexico the meat was served in a chile cooking sauce with the beans separate; however, in our Southwest it made good sense to cook all ingredients in the same pot "out on the range."

This dish is so popular in the United States that "chili cook-offs" are held annually in many communities. These contests are filled with playful "hot" disputes over whose chili recipe is the best. My only word of caution when you make chile con carne is not to be heavy-handed with the cumin. A little cumin goes a long way, and too much will overpower the other ingredients. You will find the seasoning ratio in this recipe just right.

> *Frijoles de Olla (see page 53), using red or pinto beans*
> 3 *pounds boneless chuck roast, cut into 2-inch cubes*
> 6 *ancho chiles*
> 2 *pasilla chiles*
> 1 *teaspoon dried oregano*
> ½ *teaspoon ground cumin*
> 1 *can (16 oz) tomatoes*
> 3 *cloves garlic, chopped*
> 2 *teaspoons salt*
> 2 *tablespoons lard or oil*
> 1 *onion, chopped*
> 2 *cups reserved beef broth*
>   *Garnishes: chile pequin or Japonés, crushed; chopped onion; shredded cheese*

1. Cook the Frijoles de Olla. In a large saucepan cover the meat with cold water, bring to a boil, reduce heat, cover, and simmer until tender (1½ hours). Allow the meat to cool in the broth until easy to handle.

Remove the meat, reserving the broth, and coarsely chop or shred the meat.

2. Toast the chiles on a comal or in a heavy frying pan over medium heat, turning occasionally to avoid burning. Remove and discard the stems and most of the seeds. Crumble the chiles into a blender, add oregano and cumin, and blend into a fine powder. Add tomatoes, garlic, and salt and blend briefly on low speed to an even consistency.

3. Heat the lard in a large pot. Sauté the onion until soft, add chile-tomato purée and cook 3 minutes over high heat, stirring. Add prepared meat and slowly stir in the 2 cups broth. Bring to a boil and reduce heat; drain the cooked beans and add; simmer 30 to 40 minutes.

4. Serve the crushed chiles, onion, and cheese in separate bowls as garnishes.

Serves 6 to 8.

Nothing warms the heart more than a hot bowl of Chile Con Carne y Frijoles topped with cheese. The slow cooking allows the spices to meld and the meat to become tender. This dish is perfect for a cold, wintry day.

ALBÓNDIGAS EN MOLE VERDE
Meatballs in green mole

Ground meat is seldom used in Mexico; however, *albóndigas* (meatballs) are the exception, and this meatball recipe is typically served in homes throughout Mexico.

- ½ *pound lean ground beef*
- ½ *pound ground pork or lamb*
- 2 *tablespoons bread crumbs*
- 1 *tablespoon fresh mint, minced, or 1 teaspoon dried mint, crushed*
- ½ *teaspoon salt*
  Pinch ground cumin
- 1 *egg*
- 1 *can (10 oz) tomatillos, drained*
- 1 *leaf romaine lettuce, torn into pieces*
- 1 *can (4 oz) diced green chiles (or for a hotter dish use 1 jalapeño, seeded and chopped)*
- 2 *tablespoons chopped cilantro leaves*
  Half an onion, chopped
- 1 *clove garlic, minced*
- 2 *tablespoons lard or oil*
- 3 *cups beef broth*

1. In a large bowl mix together thoroughly the beef, pork, bread crumbs, mint, salt, cumin, and egg. Form small meatballs; moisten your hands frequently with cold water to prevent the meat from sticking to them. Set meatballs aside and prepare the cooking sauce.

2. Place tomatillos, lettuce pieces, chiles, cilantro, onion, and garlic in a blender or food processor. Blend briefly into a smooth purée. Heat lard and sauté the purée for 2 to 3 minutes, stirring constantly. Slowly stir in the broth.

3. Bring the sauce to a boil, add the meatballs, and bring to a second boil. Reduce heat and simmer until the meatballs are cooked through (30 to 40 minutes).

Serves 6 to 8.

CECINA

The usefulness of cutting meat with the grain can also be seen in making *cecina*. Developed long before the advent of refrigeration, cecina is the Mexican cousin of north-of-the-border jerky. Like many other early methods of preserving (from sauerkraut to country ham), cecina provides some flavor bonuses that promise to keep it around for a long time in spite of the newer, more sophisticated methods of food preservation.

Cecina must be cut from a lean chunk of beef, such as flank steak, brisket, or rump. Cutting with the grain, make thin slices about ¼ inch apart. These slices should almost cut through the meat. Make them alternately on opposite sides so that hinges are left between the slices and, when you are done, the meat will open like a folding door. Lightly salt the elongated steak, refold, and allow to sit for half a day.

Next, hang the steak in the sun (3 hours or so in dry weather) until it is surface-dry, but not stiff. When dry, coat it with lemon or lime juice and crushed black pepper. Now rehang it in the shade for 2 or 3 days or until thoroughly dry. (Cover it with cheesecloth to protect it from insects and bring it in at night to protect it from dampness.)

Cecina is not only used as dried beef but it is also served before it is fully dried as a thin steak with a fine aged flavor. Cecina may be broiled or barbecued during the first 24 hours of hanging (assuming it's a reasonably tender cut of meat). It should be coated with oil and broiled quickly, using fairly high heat; overcooking will toughen it. The meat can be used at any time for stews; the fully dried meat makes a tasty, almost instant beef broth. Try to preserve some cecina for a high-protein, lightweight snack for backpacking and for *machaca*. Store it in a cool, dry, well-ventilated place for a short time; freeze for long storage.

MACHACA
Shredded meat

This very important *cecina* dish gets its name from the Spanish verb *machacan*, "to batter or crush." This is, of course, the method by which the meat is shredded for cooking.

To prepare machaca, roast cecina under the broiler for a few minutes on each side until hot and bubbly; cool. Shred the meat thoroughly by pounding it on a heavy chopping block or shred in small amounts in the blender until fluffy. Machaca will be more tender if you dry the fluffed meat for 10 or 15 minutes in a 200° F oven before proceeding with the recipe.

Use machaca in Machaca Con Huevos (see page 108) or as the meat in the filling recipes for Res (see page 75) or Ropa Vieja (see page 75).

PORK

LOMO EN SALSA DE ALMENDRAS
Pork loin in almond salsa

Pork steaks are a favorite cut of meat in Mexico. Cooked with ground almonds, they make a simple and quickly prepared main dish with an interesting texture.

- 2 *pounds pork loin steaks*
- 3 *tablespoons lard or oil*
  Salt and pepper
- 3 *tomatoes, finely chopped*
- 1 *onion, finely chopped*
- 1 *cup ground almonds*

1. Brown the meat in the lard and then arrange in a baking dish. Lightly salt and pepper the meat on both sides.

2. Mix together the tomatoes, onion, and almonds and place over the meat. Bake in a 350° F oven until tender (about 40 minutes).

Serves 4 to 6.

ADOBO
Pork marinated in red chile paste

Adobo is a spicy, chile-vinegar paste in which pork is marinated and then barbecued or broiled. The adobo chile paste freezes beautifully and is a timesaver when prepared ahead and frozen.

    5   dried ancho chiles
    3   dried California chiles
    2   dried pasilla chiles, if
        available
    4   cloves garlic, minced
    1   teaspoon dried oregano
    ½   teaspoon ground cumin
    ¼   teaspoon ground cloves
    1   tablespoon salt
    ½   cup white wine vinegar
    4   pounds pork (use pork steaks
        or a 4-pound pork shoulder or
        butt roast cut lengthwise into
        8 pork steaks)
        Garnishes: sliced avocado,
        thinly sliced red onion, radish
        rosettes, and salsa verde

1. Remove the stems and seeds from the chiles and discard. Place chiles in a saucepan and add water just to cover. Bring to a boil, reduce heat, and simmer for 5 minutes. Set aside to steep for 30 minutes. Drain the chiles and remove any tough pieces of peel.

2. Place chiles, garlic, oregano, cumin, cloves, salt, and vinegar into a blender or food processor and blend briefly to a textured purée. Spread the chile purée over the meat, covering both sides. Rub it in well. Cover with waxed paper and allow to season in the refrigerator for 1 to 3 days. (If necessary, the meat can be cooked immediately.)

Serves 8 to 10.

These pork steaks are first marinated in adobo and then barbecued or broiled. Garnish with sliced avocado, thin slices of red onion (separated into rings), and radish rosettes, and accompany with salsa verde. Adobo, although delicious any time of the year, is especially nice for a summer barbecue.

CARNITAS
Little meats

This method of cooking carnitas is a classic in the cuisine and is used throughout Mexico. Traditionally these little meats are made with boneless pork.

Carnitas are served as a main dish accompanied by warmed tortillas and a variety of garnishes. Each person picks up a few meat pieces in a tortilla and then adds garnishes. Carnitas may also be shredded and used to fill tacos, flautas, burritos, chimichangas, and sopes, or to top panuchos and tostadas. Smaller cubes of meat may be placed on toothpicks and served with salsa or guacamole as antojitos (hors d'oeuvres).

Carnitas are always cooked in lard with fresh orange slices. The orange supplies moisture that lowers the temperature of the lard while the interior of the meat cooks. Once this moisture has cooked away, the temperature of the lard rises, and the meat browns on the outside. The carnitas, when done, will have a dry, crispy exterior with a moist, succulent interior. There is no substitute for the lard; oil just will not work for this recipe.

  3 pounds lard (no substitute)
3½ pounds boneless pork (butt
    or shoulder), trimmed and
    cut into 3-inch cubes
    (1-inch cubes for antojitos)
    Salt
  1 small orange, sliced
  ¼ cup coarsely chopped cilantro
    (optional)
    Warmed flour tortillas
    Garnishes: As a main dish,
    serve with salsa, sour cream,
    chopped onion, cilantro,
    jalapeño slices
    As antojitos, serve with
    salsa and guacamole

1. Place the lard in a heavy, deep pot, over medium-low heat. Lightly salt the meat. When the lard has melted, place the meat, orange slices, and the ¼ cup cilantro (if used) into the pot. The melted lard must cover the meat; if it does not, add more.

2. Cook over medium-low heat, 2 to 2½ hours for 3-inch cubes, 1 to 1½ hours for 1-inch cubes. After about 30 minutes, the lard will begin to boil. Boil gently. As the moisture gradually cooks away the temperature of the lard will rise, allowing the meat to brown. If the meat has not browned at the end of the cooking time, remove the orange slices and continue to cook. As the meat browns, remove it and drain on paper towels.

3. Place the carnitas on a preheated platter or serving dish. Accompany with warmed tortillas and the garnishes. As an antojito, place each piece of meat on a toothpick and serve accompanied by salsa and guacamole for dipping.

Serves 6 as a main dish or 8 to 10 as an antojito.

Note Carnitas may be prepared in advance and reheated in a 350° F oven until heated through (10 to 15 minutes).

CUISOS—STEWS

The Mexican stews are hearty, and filled with interesting flavors and textures, the result of unusual combinations of ingredients and skillful use of spices. The following stew recipes represent some of the classics in the cuisine. Pork is the favorite meat for stews; however, Chile Verde de Res (see page 80) is an example of the use of beef in a stew.

CHILE VERDE
Green chile and pork stew

Chile verde, Mexico's classic pork stew, is a main dish popular throughout the southwestern United States as well. It will surely become one of your family favorites. Serve the chile verde accompanied by warm tortillas. Any leftovers will make delicious burritos.

  4 pounds boneless pork (butt or
    shoulder) cut into 1-inch cubes
  2 tablespoons lard or oil
    (optional)
  1 onion, coarsely chopped
  3 cloves garlic, minced
  1 teaspoon dried oregano
  ½ teaspoon ground cumin
  3 large tomatoes, peeled and
    cut into wedges
 10 mild green chiles, roasted,
    peeled, and cut into strips
    or 2 cans (7 oz each) whole
    green chiles, rinsed and
    cut into strips
  1 teaspoon salt
    Sour cream

1. Cover the meat with cold water, bring to a boil, reduce heat, cover, and simmer 40 minutes.

2. Drain meat and, in a heavy skillet over medium-low heat, render the fat from the meat, allowing the meat to brown. (Add 2 tablespoons lard or oil if the meat is too lean.) Add onion and garlic and cook until soft. Add oregano, cumin, tomatoes, chiles, and salt.

3. Cover and cook 10 minutes over medium-high heat. Reduce heat, uncover, and cook 20 minutes. Serve accompanied with sour cream.

Serves 8.

Variation This stew can be made using tomatillos rather than tomatoes. Replace the tomatoes with 2 cans (10 oz each) tomatillos, drained.

CHILE VERDE CON NOPALITOS
Pork stew with cactus

This stew is a variation of the classic chile verde with the addition of no-pales (cactus). It also uses a different approach to cooking the meat, browning it first rather than first simmering it in water. The nopales, tomatillos, and chiles provide a wonderful combination of flavors. For a hotter main dish, use jalapeños in place of the mild green chiles.

- 1½ pounds boneless pork, cut into 1-inch cubes
- 2 tablespoons lard or oil
- 1 onion, chopped
- 2 cloves garlic, minced
- ½ teaspoon dried oregano
- ¼ teaspoon ground cumin
- 1 can (7 oz) diced green chiles or 2 canned jalapeños, rinsed, seeded, and cut into small strips
- 1 can (10 oz) tomatillos, drained
- 1 jar (16 to 20 oz) nopalitos, drained and rinsed
- ½ cup water
- 2 potatoes, peeled and diced
  Salt to taste

1. In a large saucepan brown the meat on all sides in the lard. Add onion and garlic and cook until soft. Add oregano, cumin, and chiles and sauté briefly.

2. Add tomatillos, nopales, water, and potatoes. Bring to a boil, reduce heat, cover, and simmer for 30 to 40 minutes, adding small amounts of water as necessary. Check the seasoning and add salt if necessary.

Serves 6 to 8.

TINGA POBLANA
Puebla-style stew

Tingas are stews typical of the Puebla region and common throughout central Mexico. Although pork is most commonly used, veal or chicken may also be used for this stew. Tingas will often include chorizo, which dominates both the color and taste, providing a snappy flavor. Chipotle chiles (smoke-dried jalapeños) also add a unique flavor. If they are not available use canned jalapeños or, if a milder dish is desired, use diced green chiles. This tinga makes an excellent main dish. It also may be used as a filling.

- 2 pounds boneless pork (butt or shoulder), cut into 1-inch cubes
- ½ pound chorizo
- 1 onion, chopped
- 1 clove garlic, chopped
- 2 tomatoes, chopped
- 2 chipotle chiles, chopped, or 2 canned jalapeños, chopped, or 1 can (4 oz) diced green chiles
- ½ teaspoon dried oregano
  Garnishes: sliced avocado and sliced white onion, separated into rings
  Flour or corn tortillas

1. Cover the pork cubes with cold water, bring to a boil, cover, and simmer until tender (about 40 minutes). Allow the meat to cool in the broth; drain, reserving ½ cup broth. Shred the meat by using your fingers or two forks, or shred in a food processor, using the plastic blade. Place a few pieces of meat at a time into the container and process briefly (avoid shredding the meat too finely). Set aside.

2. Peel the chorizo and crumble into a large, heavy-bottomed pot (or use homemade chorizo, see page 88). Sauté for 20 minutes, until browned. Add onion and garlic and sauté until onion is soft. Add tomatoes, chiles, and oregano and cook for 5 minutes. Add shredded pork and reserved broth; simmer 15 minutes, adding small amounts of broth if necessary.

3. Garnish with avocado slices and onion; accompany with warm tortillas.

Serves 6.

GUISO DE PUERCO
Pork stew

This stew originated in the tropical regions of Mexico where there is an abundance of fruit. In this recipe meat, vegetables, and fruits are cooked together, providing a stew that has an interesting texture and a delightful flavor.

- 2 pounds boneless pork (butt or shoulder), cut into 1½-inch cubes
- 1 onion, chopped
- 2 cloves garlic, crushed
- 2 cups lentils
- 1 can (16 oz) solid pack tomatoes, puréed briefly in blender
- ⅔ cup raisins
- 3 tablespoons lard or oil
- 1 ripe plantain or 1 large, firm, underripe banana, cut into ¼-inch slices
- 1 cup fresh pineapple chunks or canned pineapple chunks, drained
- 1 teaspoon salt
  Sour cream, for garnish

1. In a large pot, cover the meat with cold water, bring to a boil, cover, and simmer 30 minutes. Add onions, garlic, lentils, tomato purée, and raisins. If necessary add more water to cover. Bring to a boil, cover, and simmer 1½ hours.

2. In a skillet heat the lard and sauté the plantain and pineapple. Add the fruit and salt to the stew and simmer, uncovered, for 10 minutes.

3. Serve garnished with sour cream.

Serves 8.

CHORIZO
Mexican sausage

The heartiness and spicy flavor of chorizo make it a delicious addition to many recipes. It is cooked and added to scrambled eggs or used in fillings for masa dishes. If you cannot find a good quality chorizo in your local markets, you can make it quickly and easily at home. Chorizo can be prepared in quantity and frozen. Freeze in 2-cup quantities (1 pound), for convenience.

> 5 dried ancho chiles
> 3 dried pasilla chiles
> 3 dried Japonés chiles
> 1 teaspoon coriander
> 1 teaspoon dried oregano, crushed
> ½ teaspoon ground cloves
> ¼ teaspoon ground cumin
> 1 tablespoon salt
> 3 tablespoons Hungarian paprika
> 6 cloves garlic, minced
> ¾ cup white wine vinegar
> 3½ pounds boneless pork (butt or shoulder), coarsely ground or finely chopped

1. Remove stems and seeds from chiles (reserving 2 tablespoons seeds). Toast chiles and reserved seeds on an ungreased, preheated comal or heavy frying pan over medium heat, turning occasionally. Cool.

2. Break the chiles into pieces and place in a blender with the seeds. Blend to a fine powder. Add coriander, oregano, cloves, cumin, salt, paprika, garlic, and vinegar; blend to mix well.

3. Add the chile purée to the ground meat and work together well with your hands. Cover the sausage and refrigerate to season, up to 2 days. Mix well twice each day. (The chorizo may be used immediately; however, the flavor will improve if it is allowed to season.) If you freeze the chorizo, allow it to season for 2 days first.

Makes 3½ pounds.

OTHER MEATS

FLAMBRES SURTIDOS
Assorted marinated cold meats

This platter of assorted meats is a meal in itself, making a wonderful summer supper or an unusual buffet. Serve accompanied by warm bolillos (Mexican dinner rolls) or French rolls, butter, and cold Mexican beer.

Meats

> 3 fresh pig's feet, each cut into 6 pieces
> 1 beef tongue
> 3 pounds chicken pieces

Meats will be cooked in separate pots and each pot will contain:

> 2 cloves garlic
> A third of an onion, cut into large pieces
> ⅛ teaspoon dried thyme
> ¼ teaspoon dried oregano (omit for chicken)
> 1 bay leaf
> 6 peppercorns

Vegetables

> 1 pound green beans
> 8 small new potatoes

Vinaigrette

> 2 cloves garlic, crushed
> ¾ cup white wine vinegar
> 2 teaspoons salt
> 1 teaspoon pepper
> 1 tablespoon Dijon mustard
> 1 cup olive oil
> 1 cup salad oil
> 2 tablespoons chopped cilantro
> 2 tablespoons capers

Garnishes

> 1 head green leaf lettuce, shredded
> Whole ripe olives
> Radish rosettes
> 4 hard-boiled eggs, sliced
> Cebolla en Lima (see page 25)
> Jalapeño chiles
> Salsa Verde (see page 22) or Salsa de Chipotle (see page 22)

1. Place the pig's feet, tongue, and chicken in separate pots, each with the suggested seasonings. Cover with cold water, bring to a boil, reduce heat, cover, and simmer 2½ hours for pig's feet, 2½ hours for beef tongue, and 30 minutes for chicken. Allow the meats to cool in the broth until easy to handle.

2. Prepare the green beans and potatoes as for Ejotes y Papas (see page 44). Prepare the vinaigrette by combining garlic, vinegar, salt, pepper, mustard, olive oil, and salad oil; shake or blend briefly in a blender. Add cilantro and capers. Mix some of the vinaigrette into each of the bowls. Refrigerate for 4 hours.

3. To assemble the meal, place the shredded lettuce on a large platter. Arrange the meats on the lettuce, place the vegetables around the edge of the platter and pour any remaining vinaigrette over all. Garnish with olives, radish rosettes, and egg slices. Serve the Cebolla en Lima (marinated onions), jalapeños, and salsa in separate bowls.

Serves 8 to 10.

CARNITAS DE CORDERO
Lamb carnitas

Traditionally carnitas are made from boneless pork (see page 86); however, lamb can also be used. Serve as you would traditional carnitas.

> 3 pounds meaty lamb necks or ribs, cut in small sections
> 1 cup water
> 1 clove garlic
> 1 bay leaf
> 2 whole cloves
> 3 whole peppercorns
> Salt
> Tortillas
> Salsa

1. Place meat, water, garlic, bay leaf, cloves, and peppercorns in a large pot; bring to a boil, reduce heat, cover, and simmer for 20 to 30 minutes.

2. Remove the meat and place in a baking pan. Lightly salt and bake in a 325° F oven until browned on all sides.

3. Place the meat pieces on a pre-heated platter or serving dish. Serve with warmed tortillas and salsa.

Serves 8.

CONEJO ENVINADO
Rabbit in white wine

Although rabbit is not always available in restaurants in Mexico, occasionally you will find such a dish as *conejo envinado*, a unique combination of chiles and tomatoes simmered with the rabbit in white wine.

> ¼ cup oil
> 3 pounds rabbit, cut into serving pieces
> 3 cloves garlic
> 1 onion, coarsely chopped
> 3 poblano chiles, roasted, peeled, and cut into strips (rajas)
> 2 large tomatoes, peeled and cut into thin wedges
> ⅛ teaspoon dried thyme
> 1 cup dry white wine
> ½ cup chicken broth
> Salt and pepper to taste

1. In a skillet, heat oil to 370° F and brown the rabbit pieces 10 minutes on each side. Remove the rabbit and set aside. Toast garlic in the oil to a golden brown; remove garlic and discard.

2. Cook onions until soft, add chiles, tomatoes, and thyme, and sauté approximately 1 minute. Slowly stir in the wine and broth. Bring to a boil, add the rabbit, reduce heat, cover, and simmer until tender (1 to 1½ hours, depending on size of the rabbit pieces). Turn the meat at least once while simmering, and baste occasionally. Check the seasoning and add salt and pepper, if necessary.

Serves 4 to 6.

BIRRIA

Birria is a fiesta in itself. This dish, often offered as a specialty in many restaurants in Mexico, is seldom seen in the United States. Although lamb is most frequently used in birria, goat is also used throughout Mexico.

Traditionally, birria is cooked in a pit, and it is still cooked for country celebrations in this way. Usually a whole lamb is cooked. The following oven-method birria has been adapted from the authentic hole-in-the-ground version. The object is to keep as much steam as possible from escaping in order to prevent any loss of flavor. Because birria is cooked in a pot, this would seem simple; however, there is naturally more steam in a well-sealed hole in the ground than in your oven, and it is necessary to make a few modificatons to achieve the same results.

> 6 dried ancho chiles
> 2 dried pasilla chiles, if available (optional)
> 1½ cups white wine vinegar
> 3 cloves garlic, crushed
> 2 teaspoons dried oregano
> 1 teaspoon salt
> 1 scant teaspoon ground cumin
> ½ teaspoon ground cloves
> 5 pounds assorted lamb pieces (shanks, ribs, necks, etc.)
> 1 cup water
> 1 bay leaf
> Small amount of masa or masa harina and water
> Garnishes: chopped onion, chopped radish, chopped cilantro, and your favorite salsa   .
> Tortillas

1. Remove stems and seeds from chiles. Place chiles in a saucepan with the vinegar, bring to a boil, reduce heat, and simmer a few minutes until soft. Place chiles and vinegar, garlic, oregano, salt, cumin, and cloves into a blender or food processor and blend briefly into a smooth paste.

2. Coat the meat pieces thoroughly with the chile paste and allow to marinate in the refrigerator for at least 4 hours. If possible marinate the meat overnight or up to 24 hours.

3. Place the water in the bottom of a large ovenproof pot (with a lid), put a low rack over the water, and place the meat pieces on the rack. Add the bay leaf. For a better seal, place cooking parchment paper over the meat. Cover with the lid.

4. Preheat oven to 350° F. Using fresh masa (or masa harina mixed with water to form a stiff dough), form a seal around the lid of the pot. Bake for 4 hours. Remove the pot from the oven and break the masa seal. The meat will be succulent and falling from the bones. Place the meat on a preheated serving platter.

5. In a bowl, combine the chopped onion, radish, and cilantro. Serve this onion mixture, salsa, and warmed tortillas as accompaniments for the meat.

Serves 8.

POULTRY

Since ancient times, wild and domestic fowl have added succulence to the Mexican menu. In the early Spanish chronicles of New Spain, numerous birds are mentioned as part of the diet of the Aztecs. There were turkeys, quail, pigeons, and many kinds of ducks and water birds.

Fowl was generally cooked by the Aztecs in covered underground pits, with a pot positioned over the hot stones to catch the drippings. The meat was covered with *mixiote*, a thin membrane from the leaf of the maguey plant. In spirit and technique, these earliest Mexican feasts are related to contemporary cuisine.

Cooking Sauces

Many of the cooking sauces of Mexico are at their best in poultry dishes. Of the hundreds of cooking sauces in the Mexican cuisine, many are specific to certain regions. Some of the cooking sauces are referred to as *moles* or *pipianes*. *Moles* are rich sauces made of spices, chiles, chocolate, and seeds. *Pipianes* are sauces made of ground nuts or seeds and spices. These sauces are further identified by the region of their origin, as in *mole poblano* (from the city of Puebla); or by color, as in mole verde (green mole); or even by the type of chile or other ingredients that are included in the sauce, as in *pipian de almendras* (almond pipian). The moles in particular are direct descendants of Aztec recipes.

The recipes here represent some of the classic cooking sauces typically used throughout Mexico.

An important key in the preparation of these traditional Mexican cooking sauces is the manner in which the sauce is thickened. Nuts or seeds are ground very fine and serve as the thickening agent. Flour is seldom used to thicken a cooking sauce, with some exceptions in the northern, wheat-growing part of Mexico. Occasionally in the United States you will find Mexican cooking sauces thickened with cornstarch, but cornstarch is not used to thicken cooking sauces in the traditional cuisine.

Cooking Notes Please note that the salt amounts given in each recipe are only a suggestion. The addition of salt will vary depending on the seasoning of the broth used and individual taste.

Some canned food products will work well in these cooking sauces: canned mild whole green chiles may be substituted when fresh chiles are not available, and canned chicken broth may be used when a busy schedule requires a convenient timesaver.

MOLE POBLANO

There are many *moles* descended from the *chilmolli* of the Aztecs, but the richest are those served with *guajolote* (the Aztec word for turkey). Of these, *mole poblano* is probably the most famous. It does not use the fresh poblano chile, but, like the chile, its name comes from the city of Puebla. A cookbook published there in 1877 gave recipes for 44 moles.

The story of the creation of mole poblano is told in many versions and probably reports a real event that occurred some 200 years ago. The sisters of Puebla's Convent of Santa Rosa, in honor of the visiting Viceroy, devised a mole of unusual (and possibly desperate) complexity, a brave combination of chiles, nuts, tomatoes, garlic, seeds, cinnamon, and chocolate. Whether through divine inspiration or devilish necessity, it was a success.

Mole poblano is traditionally served with Tamales Blancos (see page 72) or Arroz Blanco (see page 36) and accompanied by Ensalada de Noche Buena (see page 43).

MOLE POBLANO
Mole Puebla style with chicken or turkey

Mole poblano is a traditional dish throughout Mexico for the Christmas turkey or with chicken for any special occasion during the year. Just how close this recipe is to the original is hard to say. It is, however, the authentic mole poblano as served today in Mexico, an unusual combination of ingredients which, when blended together, results in a sauce of exquisite flavor.

In preparing this recipe you will experience one of the traditional cooking secrets of the Mexican cuisine: toasting each ingredient to enhance its individual flavor before blending together the ingredients. This process takes the edge off the taste of many ingredients and brings out subtle underlying flavors that would otherwise be missed.

The sauce for mole poblano can be prepared one day ahead.

⅔ cup whole almonds
6 dried mulato chiles (see Note 1)
4 dried ancho chiles
4 dried pasilla chiles
½ cup lard
8 pounds turkey or chicken, cut into serving-sized pieces (see Note 2)
    Giblets
4 cups water
1 teaspoon salt
⅓ cup sesame seed
¼ teaspoon anise seed
1 cinnamon stick
4 cloves garlic, unpeeled
¼ cup lard
1 dry corn tortilla
¼ cup raisins
¼ teaspoon ground coriander
¼ teaspoon ground cloves
3 tablespoons lard
3 ounces Mexican chocolate
3½ cups reserved chicken or turkey broth

1. Toast almonds in a 300° F oven for 30 minutes. Set aside to cool.

2. Wash chiles and remove stems and seeds. Open the chiles flat and place into a saucepan. Weight them down with a plate and cover with water. Bring to a boil and allow to cook 5 minutes over medium heat. Set aside.

3. Preheat oven to 325° F. In a large skillet, heat the ½ cup lard and brown the turkey or chicken pieces over medium heat, 10 minutes on each side. Transfer to a baking dish and bake for 50 minutes. Set aside.

4. In a saucepan, cover the giblets with the 4 cups water and 1 teaspoon salt. Bring to a boil and simmer for 30 minutes. Drain and reserve broth.

5. In an ungreased skillet, toast the sesame seed over medium heat, tossing frequently, until golden (about 3 minutes). Remove from pan, reserve 2 tablespoons toasted sesame seed and set aside. In the skillet, toast anise seed, cinnamon stick, and garlic over medium heat. Peel the garlic and set aside. In a blender, finely grind the cinnamon stick, anise, and remaining sesame seed. Set aside.

6. In a comal or heavy frying pan, heat the ¼ cup lard over medium heat and fry the tortilla until crisp and golden. (If tortilla is fresh, dry slowly in 200° F oven.) Fry the raisins briefly, to puff them. Break tortilla in pieces into the blender. Blend into fine crumbs. Add the cooled, toasted almonds and blend until fine. Remove the mixture from the blender and set aside.

7. Place in the blender the raisins, sesame seed, and cinnamon, anise, and garlic mixture. Add coriander and cloves. Drain the cooled chiles, reserving the liquid. Add to the blender 1 cup chile liquid and the chiles. Blend briefly for an even consistency. Add the almond-tortilla mixture and ½ cup of the reserved turkey or chicken broth. Blend.

8. In a large pot melt the 3 tablespoons lard. Add the chile mixture and fry 5 minutes, stirring constantly. Break the chocolate into pieces and add to the chile purée; lower the heat and cook 10 minutes to melt the chocolate, stirring constantly. Slowly stir in the remaining reserved turkey or chicken broth, bring to a boil, lower heat, and simmer for 30 minutes. If necessary add small amounts of broth or liquid from the chiles to achieve the desired consistency.

9. Add turkey or chicken pieces to mole and cook to heat through. Transfer to a serving dish and top with the reserved sesame seed or place the turkey or chicken pieces in a bakeproof serving dish, pour mole over all, cover and place in a 350° F oven to heat through (approximately 20 minutes). Remove cover, sprinkle with the reserved sesame seed, and serve.

Serves 10 to 12.

Cooking Notes

1. The mulato chile called for in this recipe is traditionally used in Mexico for the classic mole poblano. The mulato chile is similar in shape to the ancho chile but stiffer and a dark chocolate-brown color, without the reddish tint found in the ancho. Although not absolutely essential, mulatos do add an important flavor to the sauce. If this chile is unavailable, substitute additional ancho chiles or make the Shortcut Mole (see recipe at right), which uses a prepared mole paste that can be purchased in jars in markets.

2. To use leftover cooked turkey or chicken, omit steps 3 and 4 and increase the baking time in step 9 to 30 minutes.

3. Mole poblano freezes beautifully and is a real convenience when prepared ahead and frozen. Make a large quantity; it will keep successfully up to one year in the freezer. To prepare the sauce for freezing, follow steps 1, 2, 5, 6, and 7. Divide the chile purée into quantities for making a single recipe, and freeze. When ready to make mole poblano, thaw the chile purée and proceed with steps 3, 4, 8, and 9.

SHORTCUT MOLE

This simplified version of the classic mole poblano is a convenient time-saver and advantageous if the ingredients for the traditional mole poblano are unavailable. This recipe requires a prepared mole paste, which can be purchased in jars in Mexican markets here in the United States. Although this sauce is good, it doesn't have the full flavor of mole poblano made in the traditional manner.

> *8 pounds turkey or chicken, cut into serving-sized pieces (or use cooked turkey or chicken)*
> *½ cup lard*
> *2 jars (8 oz each) prepared mole poblano paste*
> *5 cups turkey or chicken broth*
> *2 tablespoons sesame seed, toasted*

1. Prepare the turkey or chicken as for Mole Poblano (see opposite page, steps 3 and 4) or use leftover cooked turkey or chicken.

2. Into a large pot, pour the oil that has separated to the top of the jar of mole paste. Heat the oil, add the paste, and fry for 3 minutes over medium heat, stirring. Slowly stir in the broth. Bring to a boil, reduce heat, and simmer 5 minutes.

3. Add the prepared turkey or chicken to the mole and cook to heat through, or place the turkey or chicken in an ovenproof serving dish and pour the mole over all. Cover and place in a 350° F oven to heat through (approximately 20 minutes). If necessary add small amounts of broth or water to maintain the desired consistency. Sprinkle with the sesame seed before serving.

Serves 8 to 10.

This version of Pipian de Almendras uses sesame seeds instead of almonds. Pipianes are cooking sauces that are thickened with ground nuts or seeds.

MOLE VERDE DE PEPITAS
Green mole with pumpkin seeds

This recipe represents the classic mole verde cooking sauce of Mexico. It uses ground pepitas (hulled, raw, unsalted pumpkin seeds) to thicken the sauce. Pepitas can be purchased in most natural food stores in the United States. Mole verde (green mole) has a base of puréed green chiles and tomatillos. The sauce is a beautiful, fresh green color and is good with turkey, chicken, duck, or pork. Serve with Arroz Blanco (see page 36), and accompany with a fruit salad or wedges of melon, pineapple, or papaya.

- 1 cup pepitas (hulled, raw, unsalted pumpkin seeds)
- 6 poblano chiles, roasted, peeled, and seeded or 2 cans (4 oz each) whole green chiles and one fourth of a bell pepper, chopped, to approximate the flavor of the poblano
- 2 cloves garlic, chopped
  Half an onion, chopped
- 2 cans (12 oz each) tomatillos, drained
- 1 leaf romaine lettuce, chopped
- ½ cup cilantro leaves
- 2 tablespoons oil
- 2 cups chicken broth
- 4 pounds cooked chicken, turkey or duck (pork may also be used in this sauce)

1. Place the pepitas in a blender or food processor and whirl until finely ground. Remove and set aside. Place chiles, garlic, onion, tomatillos, lettuce, and cilantro in a blender or food processor and blend to a purée. Add the ground pepitas and again blend until smooth.

2. In a large skillet heat the oil and sauté the purée for 3 minutes over medium heat, stirring. Slowly stir in the chicken broth, reduce heat, and simmer for 20 minutes. It is important not to allow this sauce to boil because it may separate. Add the cooked meat and simmer until the meat is thoroughly heated.

Serves 6 to 8.

MOLE VERDE CON NUECES
Green mole with nuts

This version of mole verde uses nuts as the thickening agent. The combination of the almonds, walnuts, and peanuts, toasted and ground together, lends a full-bodied flavor to this sauce. Serve with Arroz Blanco (see page 36) and a fruit salad.

- ¼ cup almonds
- ¼ cup walnuts
- ¼ cup peanuts
- 4 tablespoons oil
- 6 mild green chiles, roasted, peeled, and seeded or 2 cans (4 oz each) whole green chiles
  One fourth of a bell pepper, chopped
- 2 cups chicken broth
- 3 pounds cooked chicken, turkey, or duck (pork is also good in this recipe)

1. In a large skillet toast the nuts in 2 tablespoons of the oil. Cool and place in a blender or food processor and whirl until finely ground.

2. Place ground nuts, chiles, bell pepper, and garlic in a food processor and blend briefly until smooth. If a blender is used, add a small amount of the chicken broth to facilitate the blending.

3. Heat the remaining 2 tablespoons of oil in the skillet and sauté the chile-nut purée for 3 minutes, stirring. Slowly stir in the chicken broth and simmer for 20 minutes. Add the cooked meat and simmer until the meat is thoroughly heated. (It is important not to allow this sauce to come to a boil because it may separate.) Add small amounts of broth or water if necessary to maintain the desired consistency.

Serves 4 to 6.

PIPIAN DE ALMENDRAS
Almond pipian

Pipianes are another of the cooking sauces of Mexico. They use as their base the dried red cooking chiles and are less complicated than mole poblano. As with most of the cooking sauces, they are thickened with ground nuts or seeds. Serve with Arroz Blanco (see page 36) and a salad.

- 6 ancho chiles
- ½ cup almonds or 1 cup pumpkin seeds or sesame seeds
- 1 clove garlic, chopped
- ⅛ teaspoon ground cloves
- ⅛ teaspoon ground cinnamon
- 2 tablespoons lard or oil
- 2 cups chicken broth
  Salt to taste
- 3 pounds cooked chicken or turkey (pork or tongue is also good in this recipe)

1. Wash chiles, removing the stems and reserving 1 tablespoon of the seeds. Place chiles in a saucepan and cover with water. Bring to a boil, reduce heat to medium, and cook for 5 minutes. Set aside to steep for 30 minutes.

2. In an ungreased skillet toast almonds and chile seeds over medium heat, stirring. Cool, place in a blender, and grind very fine. Remove chiles from saucepan and add to the blender together with the garlic, cloves, and cinnamon. Blend to a smooth purée, adding a small amount of liquid from the cooked chiles if necessary to facilitate the blending.

3. In a large skillet, heat the lard and sauté the chile purée for approximately 3 minutes. Slowly stir in the chicken broth, bring to a boil, then reduce heat. Check the seasoning and add salt if necessary. Add the cooked meat and simmer until the meat is heated and the sauce has thickened.

Serves 4 to 6.

Baked in a sauce containing chopped almonds, pineapple, and grapes, Pollo Almendrado is a rich, tangy chicken dish.

POLLO ALMENDRADO
Almond chicken

This main dish recipe reflects the tropical regions of Mexico, its use of fruit providing a light, refreshing flavor. Serve accompanied by Arroz Blanco (see page 36) and a salad.

  ¾ *cup whole almonds, blanched*
  3 *pounds chicken pieces (cut-up whole chicken or chicken breasts)*
  ½ *cup crushed pineapple*
  1 *cup fresh, seedless grapes or 1 small can (8 oz) whole grapes, drained*
  1 *cup orange juice*
  1 *cup dry white wine*
  2 *tablepoons honey (only if using fresh grapes)*
  ⅛ *teaspoon ground cloves*
  ⅛ *teaspoon dried thyme Slivers of orange rind, for garnish*

1. Toast almonds in a 300° F oven for 30 minutes. Cool and grind ½ cup of the almonds in a blender until fine. Coarsely chop the remaining ¼ cup.

2. Brown the chicken pieces in the hot oil (370° F), 10 minutes on each side. Place the chicken pieces in a single layer in a shallow glass baking pan.

3. Preheat oven to 325° F. In a medium bowl combine pineapple, grapes, orange juice, wine, honey (if used), cinnamon, cloves, thyme, and almonds, and pour over the chicken. Bake for 40 minutes, basting several times. Increase oven to 350° F and bake 10 minutes longer.

4. Garnish with orange rind and serve.

Serves 4 to 6.

PESCADO Y MARISCOS— FISH AND SHELLFISH

A drive across the width of Mexico is enough to convince you that all Mexicans are seafood lovers, and for good reason; the variety of seafood is probably equaled only in the Orient.

Scrupulously fresh seafood is offered in markets across the country. Wherever transportation allows rapid delivery, there are open-front cafes serving nothing but *pescados* and *mariscos*. Seafood cocktails and entrées in coastal restaurants are so good that other choices seem silly. This seafood habit is of ancient lineage.

With good, fresh fish and shellfish, the simplest cooking methods are generally best: charcoal grill, sauté, bake, or fry it.

Mexico is long on seacoast and short on rivers and streams. The fish served in inland Mexico usually come from the ocean, though some regions do produce remarkably good fresh-water fish. Unfortunately, in the United States we seldom see the wonderful seafood dishes of the Mexican cuisine.

Each village and city along the Mexican coast has its own prized recipes; below are some representative styles and techniques.

MENU NOTES

Fish dishes are best complemented by a rice side dish (rather than the bean side dishes more commonly served with meat or masa entrées). Best choices are Arroz Blanco (see page 36) or Arroz Verde (see page 36), although any of the sopa seca recipes will work well with the fish entrées. A green salad, vegetable salad, fruit salad, or melon or papaya wedges are also good selections to round out the fish menu. Avocado or guacamole also go well with fish.

In Mexico warm bolillos (Mexican dinner rolls) and butter would accompany a fish entrée; you may substitute French rolls.

Serve dry white wine, a natural accompaniment to the fish menu, and finally, bring your meal to a close with a dessert and Mexican coffee. Flan or Pastel de Pecana (see page 118) particularly complement fish entrées, but other selections might be a fruit ice, ice cream, or capirotada de piña.

HUACHINANGO CON JUGO DE NARANJA
Red snapper with orange juice

This recipe is a favorite throughout Mexico yet is seldom served in the United States. The orange and cilantro complement each other and produce a fresh, delightful taste. Although red snapper is suggested in this recipe, any mild, firm-fleshed fish will work well.

- 2 pounds red snapper fillets
- 2 tablespoons butter
  Half an onion, finely chopped
- 2 cloves garlic, minced
- 2 tablespoons oil
- 2 cups orange juice
  Pinch ground cinnamon
- 1 small jar pimiento-stuffed green olives, drained and cut in half crosswise
- ¼ cup coarsely chopped cilantro leaves, for garnish

1. Preheat oven to 350° F. Arrange the fish in a lightly buttered baking dish. Score each fillet with a sharp knife and dot with butter.

2. In a skillet sauté the onions and garlic in the oil until soft. Add the orange juice and cinnamon. Arrange the olives on the fish and pour the orange juice mixture over all. Bake for 25 to 30 minutes, basting occasionally. Baking time will depend on thickness of the fillets; take care not to overcook.

3. Garnish with the fresh cilantro.

Serves 4.

BARBECUED FISH KEBAB

There is no better way to cook fish than over hot coals. Preheat the grill thoroughly. Use Mexican mesquite charcoal for a hotter fire and a nice and authentic aroma. Compose the kebab according to what is in season. Here we use cubes of halibut, scallops, and prawns. Serve over a bed of salsa and with yellow rice.

- 1½ pounds thick fillets of firm-fleshed white fish such as halibut, sea bass, cod, or salmon
- 8 to 10 scallops
- 8 to 10 prawns
  Salt
- ½ cup butter
- ½ cup olive oil
  Juice of 2 limes
- ¼ cup cilantro, finely chopped
- 6 green onions, finely chopped
- 2 cloves garlic, chopped
- 8 to 10 red or green jalapeño peppers
- 2 zucchinis, sliced
  Cilantro and lime wedges, for garnish

1. Wash the fish, scallops, and prawns well with cold water. Pat dry. Cut fish into 1½-inch cubes. Sprinkle fish and scallops with salt.

2. Melt butter in small saucepan over medium heat. In a medium bowl stir together melted butter, olive oil, lime juice, cilantro, green onions, and garlic. Marinate fish and scallops in mixture for ½ hour.

3. While marinating, prepare the grill. It is ready when the coals are so hot that you cannot hold your hand a few inches above them for longer than a count to four.

4. Remove fish and scallops from marinade. Prepare the skewers, alternating the fish and shellfish with jalapeño peppers and zucchini slices.

5. Grill 3 to 4 inches above the hot coals for 6 minutes, turning after 3 minutes. Baste the kebabs with the marinade while grilling. Garnish with cilantro and wedges of lime.

Serves 6 to 8.

PESCADO FRITO
Fried fish

In coast-side restaurants in Mexico, the simply prepared *pescado frito* is a favorite dish of local residents. Most restaurants will use this method for the fresh catch of the day. Any mild, firm-fleshed fish will work. Garnished with fresh lime wedges and salsa, this deceptively simple dish is magnificent. Accompany this dish with Ejotes y Papas, green beans with potatoes (see page 44), and warm tortillas and butter.

> 3 cloves garlic
> Oil 1 inch deep, for frying
> Small whole fish, scaled
> and cleaned (use 1 whole
> fish per serving)
> Flour
> Salt
> 4 fresh limes (cut 3 limes
> into wedges and thinly slice
> the other lime)
> Cebolla en Lima (see page 25)
> Salsa, choose your favorite

1. Place garlic cloves in the oil and heat oil to 370° F. When garlic is toasted golden brown, remove and discard it.

2. Score each fish by making diagonal cuts along the sides with a sharp knife. Coat the fish with flour and salt lightly. Cook the fish in the preheated oil until golden brown on one side; then turn and cook until golden on the other side, approximately 10 minutes on each side. The fish should flake easily with a fork; cooking time will depend on the size and thickness of the fish. Drain on paper towels.

3. Place the fish on a serving plate, arrange several Cebolla en Lima on each fish, top with a thin lime slice, and serve with additional lime wedges and salsa.

HUACHINANGO A LA VERACRUZANA
Red snapper Vera Cruz–style

This dish is a national classic. Although it originated in Vera Cruz, *huachinango a la Veracruzana* is served with pride throughout Mexico. The slightly exotic aroma and flavor of the spices together with the bite of the jalapeños make it a dish for even those who "don't like fish." Although red snapper is traditionally used for this recipe, any mild, firm-fleshed fish can be used. Serve with corn on the cob (see page 47) and a salad of fresh greens.

> 1 large white onion, sliced thin
> and separated into rings
> 3 cloves garlic, minced
> 3 tablespoons olive oil
> 8 tomatoes, peeled, seeded,
> and chopped
> 2 to 3 canned jalapeño chiles,
> rinsed and cut crosswise
> in thin slices
> 1 small jar pimiento-stuffed
> green olives, drained and cut
> in half crosswise
> ¼ teaspoon ground cinnamon
> Pinch ground cloves
> Juice of ½ lemon
> ½ teaspoon salt (optional)
> 3 pounds red snapper fillets
> 1 tablespoon capers, for garnish
> 2 tablespoons coarsely chopped
> cilantro leaves, for garnish

1. Preheat oven to 350° F. Sauté onions and garlic in the olive oil until soft. Add tomatoes, chiles, olives, cinnamon, cloves, and lemon juice. Simmer over low heat approximately 5 minutes. Check seasoning and add salt if necessary. Keep warm.

2. Place the fish in a single layer in a shallow baking pan and bake until easily flaked with a fork (about 15 minutes). Baking time will depend on thickness of the fillets; take care not to overcook.

3. Arrange the fish on a heated platter, spoon the sauce over the fish, and garnish with the capers and cilantro.

Serves 6.

HUACHINANGO ALMENDRADO
Red snapper with almonds

This recipe, quick and simple to prepare, provides a tasty texture contrast of almonds and fish with the fresh flavor of cilantro. Any mild, firm-fleshed fish can be used. Accompany the fish with Mexican dinner rolls called bolillos and Ensalada de Nopalitos, page 42.

> 2 small whole red snappers,
> scaled and cleaned
> ½ cup cilantro leaves, chopped
> ½ cup almonds, toasted and
> finely chopped
> 4 tablespoons butter
> Juice of 2 limes
> ½ teaspoon salt (optional)

1. Preheat oven to 350° F. Score the fish by making diagonal cuts along the sides with a sharp knife. Place fish in a baking pan. Sprinkle cilantro and almonds over the fish.

2. Melt butter, add lime juice and salt (if desired) and pour over the fish. Cover pan with foil and bake until just tender (25 to 30 minutes). Baking time will depend on the thickness of the fish.

Serves 4.

One of the most popular fish dishes, Huachinango Almendrado is cooked in a sauce of almonds, cilantro, garlic, butter, and lime.

Seviche, a colorful, nutritious, and unusual dish, is perfect to serve for lunch, as an appetizer, as a first course, or for a light supper. The fresh fish is marinated in lime juice, onions, and spices, and served chilled.

FISH APPETIZERS

SEVICHE
Marinated raw fish

Seviche is made of raw fish marinated in fresh lime juice. It is served throughout Mexico wherever fresh fish is available. When the marinating process is completed the fish is not raw in taste or texture but is slightly pickled from the lime juice. Seviche is not only refreshing and light but is especially attractive with its appealing color combinations and contrasting textures.

Serve seviche as an hors d'oeuvre, appetizer, first course, or a main course salad. To serve as a main course salad, arrange on tossed greens, with tomato wedges, cucumber slices, radish rosettes, and whole ripe olives.

Because seviche is not actually cooked, ocean fish rather than freshwater fish is recommended. Usually white ocean fish is used; however, salmon and shellfish also make delicious seviche.

> 1 pound firm white ocean fish, cut into small cubes
> Juice of 8 to 10 limes
> Half a white onion, thinly sliced and separated into rings
> 1 tomato, peeled and diced
> 2 canned jalapeño chiles, seeded and chopped
> 2 tablespoons oil
> 2 tablespoons vinegar
> 2 tablespoons chopped cilantro leaves or ½ teaspoon dried oregano
> Green leaf lettuce
> 1 avocado, peeled and sliced

1. Place the fish in a glass or porcelain bowl. Pour the lime juice over the fish, using enough juice to cover the fish, and marinate at least 4 hours or overnight. Stir occasionally to be sure all surfaces of the fish are "cooked" by the juice.

2. Add the onion, tomato, chiles, oil, vinegar, and cilantro and mix gently. Refrigerate another 2 hours.

3. Just before serving place the lettuce leaves on individual plates, arrange the seviche on top, and garnish with the avocado slices.

Serves 4 to 6.

PESCADO EN ESCABECHE
Fish in vinegar

Pescado en escabeche is not a true seviche because it is cooked; however, this pickled fish is a delicious first course or hors d'oeuvre. Another excellent way to serve it is as a main course salad; serve over tossed greens, with tomato wedges, cucumber slices, radish rosettes, and sliced avocado.

        2   pounds mild, firm-fleshed
             fish fillets, sliced
        ½   cup oil
        1   red onion, thinly sliced and
             separated into rings
        2   cloves garlic, minced
        3   mild green chiles, roasted,
             peeled, and chopped
        1   can ripe olives, drained
        2   limes, cut into thin slices
        ½   cup (or more) vinegar
        ½   teaspoon salt (optional)
             Pinch dried oregano
             Green leaf lettuce

1. Sauté fish slices in oil until golden on both sides and tender. Arrange in a glass serving dish with cover. Place onion, garlic, chiles, olives, and lime slices over the fish.

2. Mix the remaining oil in which the fish was fried with vinegar, salt, and oregano and pour over the fish. Add more vinegar if necessary to cover the fish. Refrigerate 2 to 4 days before serving.

3. To serve, place lettuce leaves on a platter or individual plates and arrange the fish mixture on top.

Serves 6.

SEVICHE DE JAIBA Y CAMARONES
Crab and shrimp seviche

This version of seviche, using crab and shrimp, gives it a special-occasion flair. Serve this dish as an appetizer for a summer barbeque or for a party. Its cool refreshing flavor and striking color combinations make this dish irresistible.

        ½   pound shrimp, peeled
             and cleaned
             Juice of 6 limes
        ½   pound crabmeat, fresh
        2   tablespoons finely chopped
             white onion
        1   tomato, peeled, seeded,
             and chopped
        1   tablespoon chopped cilantro
             leaves
        2   canned jalapeño chiles, seeded
             and chopped
             Green leaf lettuce (optional)
        1   avocado, peeled and sliced
        6   pimiento-stuffed green
             olives, sliced

1. Place the shrimp in a glass bowl. Pour the lime juice over the shrimp and marinate at least 4 hours or overnight.

2. Add the crabmeat, onion, tomato, cilantro, and chiles and mix gently. Refrigerate for 2 hours.

3. To serve, place the lettuce leaves on individual plates and arrange the seviche on top, or place the seviche in cocktail dishes. Garnish with the avocado and olive slices.

Serves 4 to 6.

SHELLFISH

Shellfish are an important part of the daily eating pattern for residents along the coastal areas of Mexico. Shrimp, scallops, abalone, crab, lobster, clams, and oysters are all favorites.

Lobster is cooked simply (usually broiled quickly over coals) and served in the shell as a main course.

Shrimp, scallops and abalone are typically sautéed in "mojo de ajo" (garlic butter) and served as a main course.

Clams and oysters (as well as shrimp, abalone, and crab) are favored for "coctels" (seafood cocktails).

Abalone (abulon), native to the Pacific Coast, is a shellfish well known and prized by gourmets and scuba divers from San Francisco to southern Mexico. It is particularly plentiful along the coasts of Baja California, where an overabundance of skindivers has not yet depleted the supply. On the West Coast it can be purchased either fresh or frozen. In its frozen state it is now being distributed throughout the United States.

The common way to prepare this delicate-flavored shellfish is to slice it into ⅜-inch slices, pound it until tender, and sauté (plain, dipped in egg, or lightly floured) it in lemon butter or garlic butter. It is important to cook only one minute on each side or the abalone will toughen.

Canned abalone can be used in seafood cocktails, as an appetizer, in sauces or pickled. Canned abalone can be purchased in Mexican markets in the United States and in stores that import Mexican goods.

These shrimps are dipped in a chile-flavored garlic butter and then broiled over hot coals for only 3 minutes. This is a quick, easy, and elegant meal. Serve with a sopa seca such as Fideo (page 36).

CAMARONES AL MOJO DE AJO
Shrimp in garlic butter

Here is a variation of *mojo de ajo* (garlic butter) used with shrimp cooked over hot coals. Serve as an appetizer or main course. Accompanied by a sopa seca such as Fideo (see page 36), warm tortillas, and a green salad, it makes a splendid meal.

> 1½ pounds medium to
>   large shrimp
>   5 tablespoons butter
>   3 cloves garlic, pressed
>   Pinch mild powdered chile,
>   unseasoned
>   1 tablespoon fresh lime juice

1. Peel shrimp, leaving the tail for a handle. Remove vein.

2. Melt the butter in a small pan. Add garlic, chile, and lime juice. Simmer 1 minute.

3. Dip each shrimp in garlic butter and place on skewers (the double-prong type of skewer will keep the shrimp flat). Broil over hot coals, basting with the remaining garlic butter, turning once and cooking only until pink (approximately 3 minutes). Take care not to overcook the shrimp or they will become tough.

Serves 4 as a main course, or 6 to 8 as an appetizer.

MARISCOS
Shellfish in garlic butter

This simple recipe is the most common method for cooking seafood in Mexico. The ingredients and brief cooking enhance the shellfish and allow its full flavor and delicate texture to be savored. Serve as a main dish. Either shrimp, scallops, or abalone can be used in this recipe.

- ¼ pound butter
- 4 to 6 cloves garlic, minced
- 3 limes
  Cilantro leaves or chopped parsley
  Use one of the following:
- 2 pounds medium to large shrimp, shelled and deveined
- 2 pounds scallops
- 6 to 8 thin abalone steaks, pounded to tenderize

1. Melt the butter in a large skillet over low heat, add the garlic, and sauté until soft. Add the juice from 1 of the limes and the shellfish. Sauté, stirring carefully. Cook the shrimp until just pink (about 3 minutes). Cook the abalone only 1 minute on each side. Cook the scallops until tender, (from 3 to 6 minutes, depending on thickness). Take care not to overcook the shellfish or they will become tough.

2. Cut the 2 remaining limes into wedges. Top the shellfish with cilantro and accompany with the lime wedges.

Serves 4 to 6.

JAIBAS RELLENAS
Stuffed crab

When crab comes into season, it's time to feast. This dish takes on a Mexican flair because the crab is mixed with tomato, garlic, onion, chile, pimiento, and olives. Serve accompanied with Arroz Verde (see page 36) and a fresh fruit salad.

- 2 tablespoons olive oil
  Half an onion, finely chopped
- 1 clove garlic, minced
- 3 tomatoes, peeled and chopped
- 1 can (4 oz) diced green chiles
- 12 pimiento-stuffed green olives, sliced
- 2 tablespoons minced parsley
- 10 ounces crabmeat, cooked and shredded
- ¼ cup white wine
- ½ cup fresh bread crumbs
- 2 tablespoons butter
- 12 small crab shells (optional)

1. Preheat oven to 350° F. In a large frying pan heat the oil and sauté onion and garlic until soft. Add tomatoes, chiles, olives, and parsley and simmer 5 minutes. Add crabmeat and wine.

2. Divide among 12 small, clean crab shells or 6 individual casseroles. Sprinkle each with bread crumbs and top with bits of butter.

3. Bake until golden (about 15 minutes), and serve.

Serves 6.

ARROZ CON JAIBAS
Rice with crab

This elegant main course dish combines rice, crab, chiles, and a subtle hint of wine. Achiote, the small, brick-red seed of the annatto tree, gives a golden yellow color and a delicate flavor to the rice, which is especially tasty and attractive served with fish.

- ¼ cup oil
- 2 tablespoons achiote
- 2 cups long-grain rice
- 1 small onion, chopped
- 2 cloves garlic, crushed
- 3 tomatoes, cut in thin wedges and halved
- 3 poblano chiles, roasted, peeled, seeded, and cut into strips or 4 mild green chiles
- 3 cups chicken broth
- 1 cup dry white wine
- 1½ pounds crabmeat

1. In a large skillet or saucepan, preheat the oil and fry the achiote over low heat. When the oil is deep orange and the seeds are dark, remove and discard the achiote.

2. Add rice and fry over medium heat until kernels are puffed and all oil is absorbed. Add onion and garlic and cook until soft. Add tomatoes and chile; cook until the tomato is soft.

3. Pour in the chicken broth and wine, bring to a boil, cover, and cook over medium heat for 20 minutes.

4. Lay the crabmeat on top of the rice mixture, cover, and simmer for an additional 20 minutes until all liquid has been absorbed. Thoroughly toss the rice to mix crab throughout.

Serves 8.

COCTELS— SEAFOOD COCKTAILS

Seafood cocktails are a delightful treat available from street vendors on almost every corner in cities and villages along the coasts of Mexico. Each order is prepared fresh "before your eyes." A variety of shellfish is available depending on the locale and season. These delicious coctels might be made from shrimp, crab, or abalone, or from clams or oysters that are freshly shucked as you wait. The seafood is chopped into small pieces and placed in a disposable cup; red onion and cucumber are diced and mixed with the seafood together with a bit of fresh cilantro. Fresh limes are squeezed over the cup, and you choose a dash of salsa from the several that are usually available.

COCTEL DE ABULON
Abalone cocktail

Although neither Worcestershire sauce nor catsup are traditional to the Mexican cuisine, both are now being produced in Mexico and are common condiments on many Mexican tables. Serve this coctel as an appetizer or first course.

> 1 can (1 lb) abalone, cut into small pieces
> 2 tablespoons Worcestershire sauce
> ¼ cup white wine
> Juice of 2 limes
> 1 canned jalapeño chile, seeded and minced
> Few cilantro leaves
> Tomato catsup
> 2 avocados, peeled and sliced

1. Mix together the abalone, Worcestershire sauce, wine, lime juice, chile, and cilantro. Add enough catsup to reach desired consistency. Cover and chill.

2. Serve in cocktail glasses and garnish with avocado slices.

Serves 6.

COCTEL DE MARISCOS
Seafood cocktail

This is the coctel typically served by the street vendors throughout the coastal towns of Mexico. Serve as an appetizer or first course.

> *Use one of the following:*
>
> Clams, raw or canned (drained), chopped
> Oysters, fresh or purchased in jar, rinsed, drained, and chopped
> Shrimp, cooked, drained, and chopped
> Abalone, fresh or canned, drained, and chopped
> Red onion, diced
> Cucumber, diced
> Juice from fresh limes
> Cilantro
> Your favorite salsa

1. Mix together the seafood, onion, cucumber, and lime juice. Add cilantro and chill.

2. Serve in cocktail glasses accompanied by salsa.

ABULON EN ESCABECHE
Abalone in vinegar

> 1 can (1 lb) abalone, thinly sliced
> Flour
> Salt
> ¼ cup olive oil
> ⅔ cup vinegar
> 1 small onion, sliced
> 1 clove garlic, pressed
> 6 peppercorns
> Pinch dried oregano
> 1 bay leaf

1. Coat the abalone slices with flour, lightly salt, and sauté in olive oil (not more than one minute on each side). Place in a covered glass or porcelain container.

2. Place vinegar, onion, garlic, peppercorns, oregano, and bay leaf in a saucepan. Bring to a boil, remove from heat, and pour over the abalone. Cover the dish and refrigerate for 2 days.

3. Serve chilled as an appetizer.

Serves 6.

CAMARONES ESCORPIONADOS CON CHILE ROJO
Shrimp with red chile

The shrimp for this recipe are cut along the underside rather than the back, causing them to curl like a scorpion when cooked. These scorpion-shaped shrimp make a wonderful appetizer or hors d'oeuvre and are a particularly nice addition to an antojito buffet. They may also be served as a main course by adding the cooked shrimp to the heated sauce and then serving on a bed of rice accompanied by avocado and melon wedges.

> 1½ pounds medium shrimp, shelled and deveined, but with tails left on
> Salsa de Chile Rojo (see page 21)

1. Split the shrimp by cutting with a sharp knife down the length of the shrimp on the underside to form a hinge.

2. Cook shrimp in boiling water until they turn pink (about 5 minutes). Do not overcook. Drain and chill.

3. Place the Salsa de Chile Rojo, either warm or chilled, in a bowl in the center of a platter and arrange the cooked shrimp around the bowl.

Serves 6 as an appetizer or first course.

Variation Mix 1 can (1 pound) abalone, cubed, with the juice of 2 limes; chill. Serve the abalone on toothpicks to be dipped in the Salsa de Chile Rojo.

Serves 6 as an appetizer.

MAIN COURSE SALADS

Mexican-style fish and shellfish make impressive and elegant main course salads for a luncheon or a summer supper. They are beautiful as well as delicious.

ENSALADA DE PESCADO
Fish salad

Prepare one of the following fish recipes:

> *Pescado filling (see page 77)*
> *Pescado en Escabeche (see page 99)*
> *Seviche (see page 98)*
> *Seviche de Jaiba y Camarones (see page 99)*
> *or use any leftover Huachinango a la Veracruzana (see page 96)*
> 1 *head green leaf or romaine lettuce*
> ½ *cup Oil and Vinegar Dressing (see page 44)*
> 3 *tomatoes, cut into wedges*
> 6 *radish rosettes*
> 1 *cucumber, scored with a fork and cut in ¼-inch slices*
> *Whole ripe olives or pimiento-stuffed green olives*
> 2 *avocados, peeled and sliced*
> *Crumbled queso fresco or feta cheese*
> 2 *limes, cut into wedges*

1. Thoroughly chill the prepared fish. Tear lettuce into bite-sized pieces and place in a bowl. Toss with dressing.

2. Place the lettuce on individual serving plates and top with the prepared fish. Arrange the tomatoes, radish rosettes, cucumber slices, olives, and avocado slices attractively on the fish. Sprinkle with crumbled cheese and serve with lime wedges.

Serves 4 to 6.

ENSALADA DE CAMARONES
Shrimp salad

This recipe calls for mayonnaise, often believed to be a French invention. However, it may actually be from Spain, named *salsa mahonesa* after the city of Mahon on the island of Minorca. It may have come to Mexico with the Spanish but is more likely to have come with the French occupation during the nineteenth century.

France apparently took the garlic out of the Spanish version; you'll note that Mexico has put the garlic back in.

> 2 *pounds shrimp, shelled and deveined*
> ¾ *cup mayonnaise*
> 3 *mild green chiles, roasted, peeled, seeded, and chopped or 1 can (4 oz) diced green chiles*
> 1 *small clove garlic, pressed*
> 2 *tablespoons minced onion*
> 1 *tablespoon chopped cilantro*
> 1 *canned jalapeño chile, seeded and chopped (optional; for a hotter taste)*
> 1 *head green leaf lettuce*
> ⅓ *cup Oil and Vinegar Dressing (see page 44)*
> 3 *tomatoes, cut into wedges*
> 3 *hard-boiled eggs, sliced*
> 6 *radish rosettes*
> *Whole ripe olives or pimiento-stuffed green olives*
> 2 *avocados, peeled and sliced*
> *Crumbled queso fresco or feta cheese*
> 2 *limes, cut into wedges*

1. Cook the shrimp briefly in boiling water just until pink (about 3 minutes). Drain and rinse in cold water. Combine the shrimp, mayonnaise, chiles, garlic, onion, cilantro, and jalapeño. Mix together and refrigerate until thoroughly chilled.

2. Reserving 6 lettuce leaves, tear the remaining lettuce into bite-sized pieces, place in a bowl, and toss with the dressing.

3. To serve, place a lettuce leaf on each serving plate. Top with the lettuce pieces and a mound of the shrimp mixture. Arrange tomato wedges, egg slices, radish rosettes, olives, and sliced avocado attractively around the shrimp. Sprinkle with the crumbled cheese and serve with lime wedges.

Serves 6.

ENSALADA DE QUESO ASADERO
Asadero cheese salad

> 1 *head green leaf lettuce, shredded*
> ⅓ *cup Oil and Vinegar Dressing (see page 44)*
> 2 *cups cooked and chilled, shrimp, crab, or flaked red snapper (you could also use the shrimp mixture from Ensalada de Camarones or any of the fish suggested for Ensalada de Pescado)*
> 8 *slices Asadero cheese (if unavailable, substitute large, round, thin slices of provolone or mozarella cheese)*
> *Guacamole (see page 40)*
> *Cebolla en Lima (see page 25)*
> *Cilantro leaves*
> 2 *tomatoes, cut into wedges*
> 4 *radish rosettes*
> *Whole ripe olives*
> 2 *limes, cut into wedges*

1. Toss lettuce with dressing and place a bed of lettuce on each plate.

2. Place ½ cup fish or shellfish in the center of each cheese slice. Roll and place on the lettuce. Make 2 per serving. Top with guacamole and garnish with Cebolla en Lima (marinated onions) and a few cilantro leaves.

3. Arrange tomato wedges, radish rosettes, and olives attractively next to the rolled cheese. Serve with lime wedges.

Serves 4.

In Mexico brunch is an event.
Egg dishes from Huevos
Rancheros (page 106) to the
Mexican Omelet (page 108) are a
splendid way to start the day.

Egg Dishes

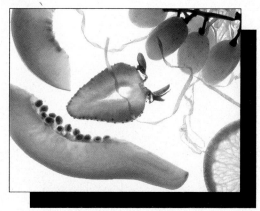

In the Mexican brunch, the emphasis falls on egg dishes. Accompanied by fresh fruits, avocados, tomatoes, chiles, Mexican sweet bread, and a side dish of rice and beans, Mexican egg dishes become much more than a simple breakfast. In addition, many of these egg dishes are perfect for lunch and dinner as well. Here you will find recipes for a multitude of egg dishes, from the traditional Huevos Rancheros to the French-influenced Mexican Omelet.

HUEVOS—EGGS

The main meal of the day in Mexico—the *comida mexicana*—is served midday. This meal is eaten at a leisurely pace and can be an eight-course affair, or, as an alternative, it can be a large, leisurely Mexican brunch. In the Mexican brunch, the emphasis falls on egg dishes. Accompanied by the appropriate garnishes, a side dish of beans or rice, tortillas, avocado and fresh fruits, *pan dulce* (Mexican sweet bread), fresh juice, Mexican chocolate or Mexican coffee, and perhaps even Mexican beer, this meal becomes a delightful feast with all of the contrasting colors, tastes, and textures so important to the cuisine. What a wonderful way to entertain!

Egg dishes, important in Mexican cuisine, are often prepared as a main dish. For many people in Mexico, turkey and chicken are too expensive to be served as everyday fare, so they are saved for special occasions. However, the eggs that are laid must be eaten and, since chickens are kept by many in the city as well as the country, fresh eggs provide a substantial amount of the protein in the Mexican diet. Eggs are seldom sold in cartons as they are here in the United States. Shoppers can be seen carrying their own egg basket to market, providing the eggs protection for the trip home.

Egg dishes are not limited to use at breakfast or brunch. They are versatile enough to be used for lunch or a light dinner as well. With the exception of Huevos Rancheros and the Mexican Omelet, all of these egg dishes make a delicious filling for tacos or burritos and are commonly used for that purpose in Mexico.

HUEVOS RANCHEROS
Ranch-style eggs

This is a hearty breakfast or brunch dish, perhaps the best known of all Mexican egg dishes.

> *Salsa Frita (see page 23)*
> *Oil ⅛ inch deep, for frying*
> *Salt*
> 6 *corn tortillas*
> 6 *eggs*
> *Sour cream and avocado slices, for garnish (optional)*

1. Prepare Salsa Frita and keep warm.

2. Heat a thin layer of oil in a skillet. Lightly salt the tortillas and fry them one at a time. Fry briefly until golden brown but not hard or crisp. Drain on paper towels.

3. Fry the eggs to suit individual taste. Sunny-side up is traditional for this recipe.

4. To serve, top each tortilla with a fried egg. Spoon the warm Salsa Frita over the egg. Garnish with a dab of sour cream and several avocado slices, if desired.

Serves 3 to 6.

Variation The eggs can be poached in the Salsa Frita. Spoon the eggs and salsa onto the fried tortillas.

HUEVOS CON CHORIZO
Mexican sausage with eggs

Chorizo, along with onions, tomatoes, and cilantro, blends with eggs to create a spicy dish. Serve with warm flour tortillas and butter.

> 1 *pound chorizo sausage*
> *Half an onion, chopped*
> 1 *tomato, chopped*
> 6 *to 8 eggs, lightly beaten*
> ¼ *cup fresh cilantro, slightly chopped*
> *Sour cream, for garnish*

1. Remove casing from sausage; crumble into a skillet. Sauté 15 to 20 minutes over medium heat. Drain excess fat.

2. Add onion and tomato and cook until soft.

3. Stir in eggs and cilantro and continue to cook until set.

4. Serve with a dab of sour cream.

Serves 4.

Note If using homemade chorizo, use 2 cups (see page 88). Homemade chorizo may require 1 tablespoon of lard or oil when cooking, as it is leaner than the chorizo purchased in the market.

HUEVOS REVUELTOS
Mexican-style scrambled eggs

This is a quick weekend breakfast or, with the addition of refried beans, hot tortillas, and a melon wedge, an excellent brunch.

> 3 *tablespoons butter*
> 1 *large tomato, peeled and chopped*
> 3 *tablespoons finely chopped onion*
> 3 *canned mild green chiles, seeded and chopped*
> 6 *eggs, beaten*
> *Salsa and avocado slices, for garnish*

1. Melt butter in a skillet over medium heat and sauté tomato, onion, and chiles until onion is soft.

2. Add eggs and scramble. Cook until set.

3. Serve with salsa and avocado slices.

Serves 3.

Chile, onion, and avocado add zest to these Mexican Scrambled Eggs. Served with fresh fruit salad, warm buñuelos or tortillas, and coffee.

HUEVOS CON FLOR DE CALABAZA
Eggs with squash blossoms

Squash blossoms add color and flavor to this egg-and-cheese dish. Serve with fresh fruit and churros or buñuelos.

- 1 pound squash or pumpkin blossoms
- 3 tablespoons butter
  Half an onion, finely chopped
  Sprig of epazote, if available
- 1 tomato, chopped
- 8 eggs
  Queso fresco (Mexican cheese), crumbled (optional)

1. Wash and chop the blossoms.

2. Melt butter in a skillet and gently sauté blossoms, onions, and epazote until onions are soft. Add tomato and cook until soft. Remove the epazote and discard.

3. Add eggs and stir. Cook until set.

4. Top each serving with queso fresco, if desired. Garnish with whole squash blossoms.

Serves 4 to 6.

HUEVOS CON NOPALES
Eggs with cactus

The succulent flavor of the cactus, somewhat like that of green beans, adds unusual flair to this egg dish.

- 3 tablespoons butter
  Half an onion, finely chopped
- 1 tomato, chopped
- 1 cup cooked nopales (see page 12) or canned nopales, drained and rinsed
- 8 eggs, beaten
  Few cilantro leaves
  Queso fresco (Mexican cheese), crumbled (optional)

1. Melt the butter in a skillet over medium heat and sauté the onion, tomato, and nopales. Cook until onion is soft.

2. Add eggs and stir. Cook until set.

3. Stir in cilantro and serve. Top each serving with queso fresco, if desired.

Serves 4.

MACHACA CON HUEVOS
Machaca with eggs

This is a meaty egg dish that can be served for breakfast, lunch, or dinner. Serve with warm tortillas and butter.

- Half an onion, chopped
- 1 tablespoon oil
- 2 tomatoes, chopped
- 1 jalapeño chile, seeded and diced or ¼ cup canned diced green chiles
- 2 cups shredded machaca (see page 84)
- 1 cup water
- 4 eggs, beaten
  Salsa, sour cream, and avocado slices, for garnish
  Tortillas

1. In a skillet sauté onion in heated lard or oil until soft. Add tomatoes and chiles and cook until soft.

2. Add machaca, cook and stir until brown and dry. Add the water and cook until thick.

3. Add eggs and stir. Cook until set.

4. Serve with salsa, sour cream, avocado slices, and heated tortillas.

Serves 4.

MEXICAN OMELET

Although perhaps never seen on a menu in Mexico, how could we resist! The cuisines of Mexico and France blended in yet another way.

For each omelet

- 1 tablespoon butter
- 2 to 3 eggs, beaten
- 1 to 2 thin slices Colby or jack cheese
- 1 mild green chile, roasted, peeled, cleaned, seeded, and cut in half lengthwise or 1 canned whole green chile, seeded and cut in half
  Garnishes: salsa, sliced avocado, sour cream, fresh cilantro

1. In an omelet skillet, melt butter over medium heat until it foams. Add eggs and cook until almost set.

2. Lay the cheese slices on one half of the omelet and top with the chile halves, placing them in a single layer.

3. Fold the omelet in half by folding the unfilled side over the cheese and chile. Cook until cheese is melted and eggs are set.

4. Slide the omelet onto a serving plate. Top with a spoonful of salsa, one or two slices of avocado, a dab of sour cream, and a few cilantro leaves.

Serves 1.

CHILAQUILES

Chilaquiles are corn tortillas cut into wedges and simmered in a sauce. In Mexico, chilaquiles are a favorite on the breakfast and brunch menu. They can be served either with or without the addition of eggs, both versions being typical. There is, however, no need to limit chilaquiles to breakfast or brunch, as this dish also adapts nicely to a luncheon or family dinner.

Cooking Notes

Chilaquiles are a wonderful use for leftover or stale corn tortillas. Fresh tortillas do not work well and purchased tortilla chips will not work at all. A tough, chewy texture is necessary to prevent the tortilla pieces from breaking up as they simmer in the sauce.

To cut tortillas into wedges, stack them together flat and cut the stack into sixths or eighths, as though you were cutting a pie. Since dry tortillas are sometimes difficult to cut into wedges, cut leftover tortillas while still fresh, bag them in plastic, and freeze until there are enough for the recipe. Thaw frozen tortillas in a single layer and if necessary blot off any moisture (from freezing) with paper towels before frying. If you are starting with fresh tortillas, follow the instructions given in the recipe for drying the tortillas.

Fry the tortilla pieces by placing as many as will fit in a single layer in the skillet at one time; turn once, cooking only until tough and chewy, not crisp. This is one recipe where the use of lard rather than oil does make a difference in achieving the ethnic flavor typical of the final dish. Oil will also work, however, so feel free to use your preference.

Once the tortilla pieces have been placed in the sauce, cook the chilaquiles until the liquid has been absorbed. The finished dish should have the texture of a casserole.

CHILAQUILES
Tortilla wedges simmered in chile broth

    1 dozen corn tortillas
       Lard or oil ¼ inch deep,
       for frying
       Salt
       Half an onion, chopped
    1 clove garlic, minced
    1 tablespoon oil
    1 cup salsa
 1½   cups chicken broth
    4 to 6 eggs, beaten (optional)
       Garnishes: fresh cilantro,
       crumbled queso fresco
       (Mexican cheese), sour cream,
       avocado slices, chopped green
       onion, radish rosettes

1. Cut tortillas into wedges by stacking together flat and cutting the stack into sixths or eighths, as though cutting a pie. If using fresh tortillas, spread the cut pieces in a single layer on a baking sheet and allow to air-dry, or dry in a 200° F oven for approximately 20 minutes.

2. In a skillet melt the lard (or heat the oil to 400° F). Lightly salt the tortillas and fry until hardened, but not brown and crisp. Drain on paper towels and set aside.

3. In a large pot, sauté onion and garlic in the 1 tablespoon oil until soft. Add salsa and cook briefly. Add broth and bring to a boil.

4. Add the tortilla wedges, reduce heat, and simmer 5 to 8 minutes, scraping the bottom often. Take care not to break up the tortilla pieces. Stir in eggs (if used) during the last few minutes, and cook until set.

5. Serve the garnishes separately.

Serves 4 to 6.

CHILAQUILES CON CHORIZO
Tortilla wedges simmered in broth with chorizo

    1 dozen corn tortillas
       Lard or oil ¼ inch deep,
       for frying
       Salt
    ½ to 1 pound chorizo sausage
       Half an onion, chopped
    1 clove garlic, minced
    2 tomatoes, chopped
 1½   cups chicken broth
    4 to 6 eggs, beaten (optional)
       Garnishes: fresh cilantro,
       crumbled queso fresco
       (Mexican cheese), sour cream,
       avocado slices, chopped green
       onion, radish rosettes

1. Cut the tortillas into wedges by stacking them together flat and cutting the stack into sixths or eighths, as though cutting a pie. Spread the cut wedges in a single layer on a baking sheet and allow to air-dry, or dry in a 200°F oven for approximately 20 minutes.

2. In a skillet melt the lard (or heat the oil to 400° F). Lightly salt the tortillas and fry until hardened, but not browned or crisp. Drain on paper towels and set aside.

3. Remove casing from sausage and crumble into a large pot. Sauté 15 to 20 minutes over medium high heat. Drain excess fat. Add onion, garlic, and tomato and cook until soft. Add broth and bring to a boil.

4. Add tortilla wedges, reduce heat, and simmer 5 to 8 minutes, scraping the bottom often, taking care not to break up tortilla pieces. Stir in eggs (if used) during the last few minutes and cook until set.

5. Serve the garnishes separately.

Serves 4 to 6.

<u>Note</u> If using homemade chorizo, use 1 to 2 cups (see page 88). It may be necessary to use 1 tablespoon lard or oil when cooking homemade chorizo as it is leaner than chorizo purchased in the market.

Fresh fruits, sweets, and beverages are special treats in Mexican cuisine. You will find a wide array of refreshing ideas for dessert in this chapter.

Sweets & Beverages

Pre-Hispanic Mexicans made
very few cakes, candies,
and desserts, preferring the
natural sweetness of their
native fruits. Over time the culture
has embraced and elaborated
upon many desserts brought to it
from other countries, yet
the incredible variety of fruits
continues to be a favorite
basis for desserts and beverages.
Here you will find recipes
for ice creams, licuados, cakes and
other baked goods, candy,
and more.

This colorful, fresh Plato de Frutas, made from a multitude of fruits in season, is sprinkled with ground chiles for a little added zip. This dish can be served as an appetizer, salad, or even dessert.

FRUITS AND DESSERTS

Desserts, as such, were not a part of the native culture of Mexico. The cakes, custards, and pastries that now compete with the luscious fruits of the Mexican table were introduced by the Spanish nuns. These were usually served as special treats created for religious holidays or other important occasions. Most Mexican desserts and sweets are modifications of Spanish and French desserts. Many of them even preserve their Spanish names, although many, due to the inclusion of native fruits, must be considered truly Mexican. Fresh fruits and melons are sold from small carts by street vendors throughout Mexico from early morning until late at night. Mangoes, placed on sticks and peeled and sculptured with a knife to resemble flowers, are decorative in the vendor's cart, and exemplify the artistic flair used to present food in Mexico; and there is no easier or more practical way to eat this ripe, juicy fruit.

Most of the fruits and melons sold by the street vendors—coconuts, mangoes, oranges, papayas, pineapples, cantaloupes, honeydew melons and watermelons—are available in the United States. The root vegetable jicama, another mainstay of the fruit vendor's cart, is also becoming increasingly available.

PLATO DE FRUTAS
Fruit plate

This combination of fruits is the typical mixture served by the street vendor in Mexico. It makes an unusual first course or hors d'oeuvre. Although it is not necessary to use all the fruits listed, the more fruits you use, the more authentic and tasty the dish will be. The lime and seasonings make a refreshing complement to the fruit. The amount of each fruit you use depends upon your own taste and also the availability of the fruits in season.

> Watermelon
> Cantaloupe
> Honeydew melon
> Mango
> Papaya
> Fresh pineapple
> Fresh coconut
> Jicama
> Garnishes: Limes, salt, and ground unseasoned mild red chile

1. Remove seeds and rind from watermelon, cantaloupe, honeydew melon, mangoes, and papaya; peel pineapple and jicama; crack coconut and peel away brown inner skin. Cut all fruit into bite-sized pieces and mix together.

2. Serve on a large platter with cocktail picks or arrange on individual plates as a first course.

3. Squeeze the fresh limes over the fruit and sprinkle small amounts of salt and ground chile over the fruit to taste.

The number of servings will depend upon the variety and quantity of fruits used.

PLÁTANOS
Plantains or bananas

In Mexico bananas are available in a variety of sizes, shapes, and colors. The eating banana is typically short and yellow or reddish. The cooking banana, called plátano (plantain), is slightly larger, longer, and thicker than our typical banana. Although you may buy plantains in their green, yellow, or black stages, they are not ready to cook until the skin is entirely black and the plantain is soft to the touch. Green plantains will ripen quickly in a warm room. Plantains are becoming increasingly available in U.S. markets, but should you be unable to locate them, you may substitute regular bananas in these dessert recipes.

PLÁTANOS DULCES
Sweet bananas

> 3 plantains (or large bananas)
> 2 tablespoons butter
> 2 tablespoons brown sugar
> Dash ground cinnamon
> ¼ cup brandy
> 1 cup whipping cream
> Sugar
> Vanilla extract

1. Peel plantains and cut in half lengthwise. Sauté in butter until golden and tender. Sprinkle with brown sugar and cinnamon, add brandy, and simmer gently until brandy is absorbed.

2. Whip cream until it is spoonable but not stiff. Add sugar and vanilla to taste.

3. Serve plantains warm topped with the whipped cream.

Serves 3 to 4.

PLÁTANOS BORRACHOS
Drunken bananas

> 3 plantains (or large bananas)
> ¼ cup flour
> ¼ cup confectioners' sugar
> 2 tablespoons butter, melted
> 1 orange, peeled and sliced
> ½ cup rum
> Juice of 1 lemon
> 1 tablespoon granulated sugar
> ¼ cup water

1. Preheat oven to 350° F.

2. Mix together flour and confectioners' sugar.

3. Peel plantains. With a pastry brush coat them with butter; then roll each plantain in the flour mixture.

4. Place plantains in a buttered shallow baking dish. Arrange orange slices over plantains. Combine rum, lemon juice, granulated sugar, and water; pour over the fruit.

5. Bake for 25 minutes.

Serves 6.

HELADOS Y NIEVE—
ICES AND ICE CREAMS

Going to the ice cream shop in Mexico is a particular treat and is practically a national pastime. Each shop usually makes its own fruit ices and ice cream, and you may purchase ices or ice cream on sticks, in cones, in carry-away cups, or in hand-packed containers.

The fruit ices are particularly fine textured and the ice creams are rich and creamy. Both ices and ice creams come in a variety of flavors, everything from the unusual—tamarindo, mango, papaya, watermelon, and coconut—to the more familiar—chocolate, vanilla, nut, pineapple, banana, and strawberry. All are made from fresh ingredients and it is not uncommon to find an occasional seed in your cone or container.

HELADO DE MANGO
Mango ice

    3 fresh mangoes, peeled and
       sliced or 2 cans
       (15 oz each) sliced,
       sweetened mango
       Juice of 1 lime
    ½ cup sugar
    7 pounds coarse crushed ice
       Rock salt

1. If using canned mangoes, drain mangoes, reserving the liquid. Place mango pieces and lime juice into a blender. Blend until smooth.

2. Measure the mango pulp. Add an equal amount of water and sugar. Mix well.

3. Freeze in an ice cream maker following the manufacturer's directions. Ices require approximately one fourth more rock salt for the brine than does ice cream (1¼ parts rock salt to 4 parts ice).

4. Serve in chilled serving bowls.

Makes approximately 4 cups.

Note Although it is not necessary to season the mango ice (allow the mango ice to set), seasoning does give a better texture. To season: Remove the ice cream container. Take out the paddle and replace the lid. Drain the liquid brine from the ice cream maker. Replace the covered ice cream container and repack with the same ratio of rock salt to ice, completely covering the container. Top with newspapers. Allow to season from 20 minutes to 2 hours.

NIEVE
Ice cream

For a richer ice cream, scald the half-and-half and chill, before proceeding with the recipe or use 2 cups half-and-half and 2 cups whipping cream instead of the 4 cups half-and-half called for. By adding various fruits, nuts, or flavorings (variations follow) you can duplicate the typical ice cream found in Mexico.

    3 eggs
    ¾ cup sugar
    1½ tablespoons vanilla extract
    4 cups half-and-half
       Pinch salt
    10 pounds coarse crushed ice
       Rock salt

1. In a large bowl whisk the eggs until blended. Add sugar and whisk until thickened. Stir in vanilla. Slowly whisk in half-and-half and salt.

2. Freeze in an ice cream maker following the manufacturer's directions. Use a ratio of 1 part rock salt to 4 parts ice.

3. Serve in chilled serving bowls.

Makes 1½ quarts ice cream.

Note Although seasoning the ice cream is not necessary, it does make a better tasting ice cream. See note above.

Variations

Nuts Add ⅓ cup finely ground and ⅔ cup coarsely chopped nuts to basic ice cream recipe 10 minutes into the freezing process. Use almonds, walnuts, hazelnuts, or pecans—either raw or toasted. (To toast, place whole nuts in a skillet with 2 tablespoons butter and cook over medium heat, stirring frequently, for approximately 8 minutes. Cool before grinding and chopping.)

Strawberry Wash and stem berries, sprinkle with 2 tablespoons sugar, and mash. Add 1½ cups mashed berries to basic ice cream recipe 10 minutes into the freezing process.

Fruit pulps Use bananas, mangoes, papayas, pineapple, or peaches. Peel fruit and purée in a blender. Add 2 cups of puréed fruit pulp to basic ice cream recipe 10 minutes into the freezing process. If desired, ⅓ cup chopped fruit may be stirred into the ice cream once the freezing has been completed. Add the juice of half a lemon to fruits that will discolor—bananas and peaches—if you prepare them ahead of time.

Coconut Add ¾ cup finely shredded unsweetened coconut to the basic ice cream recipe 10 minutes into the freezing process.

Chocolate In a small saucepan over low heat, melt 8 ounces semisweet chocolate squares in 1 cup half-and-half. Stir frequently until creamy and smooth (approximately 8 minutes). Allow to cool. Proceed with basic ice cream recipe, reducing the vanilla to 2 teaspoons. Stir chocolate into egg mixture and slowly stir in the remaining 3 cups half-and-half. Strain into the ice cream container and freeze.

Homemade Nieve (ice cream) adorned with chocolate curls, and mango and strawberry helados (ices) make wonderful desserts.

HELADO DE FRESCA
Strawberry ice

    3 cups water
    ¾ cup sugar
    4 cups strawberries
       Juice of 1 lime
    10 pounds coarse crushed ice
       Rock salt

1. Place water and sugar in a saucepan, bring to a boil over medium heat, and cook for 5 minutes. Chill. Wash and stem berries. Place berries and lime juice into a blender or food processor and purée until smooth.

2. Measure the berry purée and blend with an equal amount of the chilled syrup.

3. Freeze in an ice cream maker following the manufacturer's directions. Ices require approximately one fourth more rock salt for the brine than does ice cream (1¼ parts rock salt to 4 parts ice).

4. Serve in chilled serving bowls.

Makes 4 cups.

Note Although seasoning the ice is not necessary, it does improve the texture. See note on page 114.

THE MEXICAN BAKERY

Very little baking is done in the Mexican home because each city neighborhood and every small town has its own bakery. In the smallest towns, however, you may have to inquire where to find the baker because villagers often don't put up signs. The baker is a respected professional, addressed as El Maestro, and has an appreciative but critical clientele. Each bakery usually has several bakes each day, and you must time your purchases to coincide with the emergence of your favorite items from the oven. Making a purchase in the Mexican bakery is an experience in itself. You first pick up a serving tray and a pair of tongs, supplied at the counter; then you walk past shelves or racks of the freshly baked sweet breads and cookies, making your selection. What a temptation! You'll want to try them all.

Even the smallest bakeries offer *pan dulce* in many sizes and shapes and with many different dry toppings. Most bakeries also make cream-filled puff pastries, pumpkin- and pineapple-filled empanadas, large cookies, cheese- and fruit-filled tarts, and the bolillo, a dinner roll that is somewhat like a hard-crusted sweet French dinner roll. Pies, as we know them, are not a part of the Mexican cuisine.

Because most of us are not fortunate enough to have a Mexican baker close by, we have adapted for home use recipes for the most popular Mexican bakery items.

PAN DULCE
Sweet bread

Thanks to Lee Lampo, a bread specialist and close friend, this classic pan dulce recipe has been converted to a cold-rise technique to make it convenient for the busy home baker.

Because pan dulce is prepared and then refrigerated for up to 24 hours before baking, you can make it in advance and still have fresh-from-the-oven sweet rolls.

The pan dulce, with its slightly sweetened breadlike texture, is a perfect accompaniment to any breakfast or brunch menu.

    3½ cups flour
    2 packages active dry yeast
    1 teaspoon salt
    ½ cup sugar
    ½ cup powdered milk
    2 tablespoons shortening
    1 egg
    1¼ cups warm tap water

Topping

    ½ cup butter
    ½ cup sugar
    1 egg yolk
    1 teaspoon ground cinnamon
       or vanilla extract
    ⅔ cup flour

1. Stir together 1 cup of the flour, the yeast, salt, sugar, and powdered milk. Add shortening, egg, and hot water. Beat at medium speed with an electric mixer for 2 minutes. Add another cup of flour and beat at high speed for 2 minutes. Stir in remaining flour and mix well.

2. Turn onto lightly floured board. Dough will be soft and sticky. Do not knead but gently turn dough several times with a spatula to lightly coat with flour. Cover loosely with plastic wrap and allow to rest 20 minutes. Meanwhile, grease 2 baking sheets and make topping.

3. With floured hands, divide dough into 12 pieces and shape into round, flat buns. Place on greased baking sheets.

4. Sprinkle equal amounts of topping over each bun and press lightly into dough.

5. Loosely cover rolls in plastic wrap and refrigerate 4 to 24 hours. Remove from refrigerator, uncover, and let stand while preheating oven to 400° F. Bake for 15 minutes.

Makes 12 rolls.

Topping Cream butter and sugar. Add egg yolk and cinnamon and blend. Add flour and mix well. Mixture will be crumbly.

DULCES DE JICAMA Y COCO
Jicama and coconut candy

    1 small jicama, peeled
       and coarsely grated
    1 cup unsweetened
       shredded coconut
    ½ cup orange juice
    1 cup sugar

1. Mix together jicama, coconut, orange juice, and sugar in medium saucepan and cook over low heat, stirring constantly, until the liquid thickens and mixture clings to a spoon. Remove from heat.

2. Form little mounds with a teaspoon or with your hand on a piece of foil. Allow to cool.

Makes 25 to 30 candies.

Going to a Mexican bakery is a special treat. Each one offers something new and different, but in just about every one you will find pans dulces (sweet breads) in a variety of shapes, and empanadas filled with custard.

Finely ground nuts constitute a major part of the dry ingredients in this single-layer glazed cake. You'll find this Pastel de Pecana irresistible.

PASTEL DE PECANA
Pecan cake

The *pastel de pecana* offers an excellent example of the French influence in much of Mexican baking. You'll find that this rich and satisfying cake will quickly become a favorite company dessert.

- *4 eggs, separated*
- *½ cup unsalted butter, melted and cooled*
- *½ teaspoon vanilla extract*
- *⅔ cup sugar*
- *Pinch salt*
- *⅔ cup pecans, finely ground in blender*
- *⅓ cup flour*

Honey Glaze

- *2 tablespoons butter*
- *½ cup honey*

1. Preheat oven to 350° F (325° F for glass or dark metal pans). Lightly butter and flour an 8-inch cake pan.

2. In a small bowl beat egg yolks, butter, and vanilla. Add ⅓ cup of the sugar and beat until thick and creamy.

3. In a large bowl beat egg whites with salt until frothy. Continue to beat, adding the remaining sugar, 2 tablespoons at a time, until stiff peaks form. Fold one third of the stiff whites into the yolk mixture to lighten it. Gently fold the yolk mixture into the remaining whites until fully incorporated.

4. Combine nuts and flour and sift one third at a time over the egg mixture, folding gently after each addition. Any nut pieces too large to sift may be folded in at the end or reground in the blender and sifted in. Pour batter into prepared cake pan.

5. Bake for 30 minutes. Let stand 10 minutes, turn cake out onto a wire rack, top side up, and cool for 1 hour. Glaze.

6. To cut neatly through the sticky glaze, use a sharp knife warmed in hot water and dried.

Serves 6 to 8.

Honey Glaze

1. In a saucepan melt butter over medium heat, stir in honey and bring to a frothy boil. Reduce heat and boil 3 minutes.

2. Cool slightly and pour over the cake while the glaze is still warm. Allow glaze to drip down the sides.

Variation: Apricot Glaze

> ½ cup apricot jam
> 2 tablespoons sugar

1. Place jam and sugar in a saucepan. Bring to a boil and cook for 3 to 5 minutes over medium heat.

2. Cool slightly and pour over the cake, allowing glaze to drip down the sides.

MEXICAN WEDDING COOKIES

This festive shortbread cookie is a favorite throughout Mexico.

> 2 cups flour
> 1⅓ cups confectioners'
>   sugar, sifted
> 1 cup finely chopped pecans
>   Pinch salt
> 1 teaspoon vanilla extract
> 1¼ cups unsalted butter, softened

1. Preheat oven to 350° F. In a medium bowl combine flour, ⅔ cup of the sugar, the nuts, and salt. Stir in vanilla.

2. Work the butter into the mixture until it forms a cohesive ball.

3. For each cookie pinch off about 1½ tablespoons dough and form it into a ball, using either your hands or two teaspoons. Shape about 1½ tablespoons dough into a ball. Place balls on a greased baking sheet and flatten them slightly with a spoon. Bake until lightly browned, about 30 minutes.

4. Allow the cookies to cool on a wire rack. Dust them generously with the remaining confectioners' sugar.

Makes 25 to 30 cookies.

Mexican Wedding Cookies add a festive and elegant touch to any party. Serve with Mexican coffee or some cool fruit drinks.

Delicate Flan, a classic Mexican dessert, is stunning displayed on a silver platter and garnished with persimmons and mint.

FLAN
Caramel-coated custard

Flan is most definitely the classic dessert of Mexico. Introduced by the Spanish, it also has a French counterpart in crème caramel. This satiny smooth flan melts in the mouth and is a rich yet light ending to a special meal.

Caramel

½ cup sugar
2 tablespoons water

Custard

2 cups milk
⅓ cup sugar
4 eggs
1 teaspoon vanilla extract

1. Preheat oven to 350° F.

2. *For the caramel:* Place sugar and water in a small saucepan and bring to a boil over medium-high heat. Continue cooking until it turns light brown (8 to 10 minutes). Pour into a 1-quart, smooth-surfaced mold (or 6 individual molds), turning the mold quickly in all directions to coat the bottom and the lower sides.

3. *For the custard:* Place milk, sugar, eggs, and vanilla in a blender. Blend 1 minute on medium speed. Pour into mold and place mold in a larger pan. Pour warm water into the larger pan halfway up the sides of the mold. (This is known as *baño de Maria*—Mary's bath.)

4. Bake for about 1 hour (40 minutes for individual molds). Check occasionally during baking to be sure the baño de Maria does not boil. If it boils, reduce oven heat slightly; however, do not reduce below 300° F.

Test for doneness by inserting a kitchen knife only halfway into the custard, making sure not to pierce the bottom. The custard is done when the knife comes out clean. Cool 1 hour; then refrigerate at least 3 hours.

5. Unmold by running a kitchen knife around the edge of the flan. Place a serving dish over the mold and invert it to unmold.

Serves 6.

EMPANADAS
Turnovers

This Mexican pastry is buttery rich and slightly sweet. The creamy pumpkin or pineapple filling makes this pastry almost into a morning meal. Empanadas are fun to bake and at their best when fresh from the oven.

2 cups flour
2 tablespoons sugar
¾ cup cold butter, cut into small pieces
1 egg, separated
¼ cup ice water
Calabaza or Piña filling (at right)

1. Preheat oven to 400° F.

2. Stir together flour and sugar and work in butter with pastry blender. Beat together egg yolk and the water; add gradually to flour mixture and mix well.

3. Divide dough in half for easier handling and turn onto a lightly floured board. Roll each ball of dough out thin. Cut dough into 4-inch circles.

4. Fill each circle with approximately 1 tablespoon filling, fold in half, and pinch edges to seal; then flute the edges. Place on an ungreased baking sheet, brush the tops with the slightly beaten egg white, and bake for 15 minutes.

Makes 16 empanadas.

Calabaza
Pumpkin filling

2 cups canned pumpkin
½ cup brown sugar or 3 piloncillo (Mexican raw sugar cones)
½ teaspoon anise seed or coarsely ground nutmeg

1. Place pumpkin, sugar, and anise seed in a saucepan. Cook over medium heat for 20 minutes. Cool.

2. Use as a filling for Empanadas, left.

Makes 2 cups.

Piña
Pineapple filling

1 can (20 oz) unsweetened pineapple chunks
2 tablespoons cornstarch
3 tablespoons sugar
½ cup sliced almonds
1 cup unsweetened shredded coconut
Sugar to coat

1. Drain pineapple and reserve liquid. Cut pineapple chunks in half. Add water to the reserved liquid to make ¾ cup.

2. In a saucepan combine liquid and cornstarch; stir to blend. Add sugar and pineapple chunks; bring to a boil over medium heat, stirring constantly. Reduce heat and simmer until thickened.

3. Stir in almonds and coconut. Cool.

4. Use as a filling for Empanadas, left. Roll Empanadas in sugar while still warm.

Makes 2 cups.

CAPIROTADA
Mexican bread pudding

Although bread pudding is a traditional Lenten dessert, it is also served in Mexican homes at other times, but especially in the winter. The combination of ingredients is unusual, with the cheese providing a unique flavor.

> 1 loaf French bread, sliced crosswise into ½-inch-thick slices
> 6 tablespoons butter
> 2 cups brown sugar or 12 piloncillo (Mexican raw sugar cones)
> 1 cinnamon stick
> 4 cups water
> ¼ cup dry sherry (optional)
> 1 cup sliced almonds
> ¼ cup whole almonds
> ⅔ cup raisins
> 1 pound jack cheese, grated

1. Place the bread slices in a 200° F oven until thoroughly dried (about 15 minutes). Remove bread and increase oven to 350° F.

2. Melt 2 tablespoons of the butter in a skillet, add bread slices a few at a time, and sauté until lightly browned, adding more butter as needed.

3. Prepare a syrup by placing sugar, cinnamon, and the water in a small saucepan. Bring to a boil, reduce heat, and simmer 15 minutes. Stir in sherry (if used) and set aside.

4. In a 4-cup shallow, buttered baking dish, layer the bread slices, sliced almonds, raisins, and cheese. Repeat. Sprinkle top with the whole almonds. Slowly pour the syrup evenly over all and bake, uncovered, for 40 minutes. Serve hot or cold.

Serves 8.

CHURROS
Mexican crullers

Churros were introduced to the Mexican cuisine by the Spanish and have become traditional fare in Mexico. The churro stand laden with these freshly cooked, golden sweet pastries is a common sight at all festivals.

Churros are made of a heavy dough forced through the ornamental opening of a *churrera* (a special utensil something like a heavy cake decorator). A wooden plunger is used to push long strips of dough into hot oil. You can substitute a pastry bag with a No. 6 star tip or a cake decorator fitted with the largest-holed tip for the churrera.

The hint of fresh lime in the heated oil is traditional and adds zest to the pastry. Churros are especially good served with Café de Olla and Chocolate Mexicano (see pages 123 and 124).

> 1 lime, quartered
> Oil ½ inch deep, for frying
> 1 cup water
> ½ teaspoon salt
> 1 tablespoon sugar
> 1 cup flour
> 1 egg
> Sugar

1. Place the lime pieces into the oil and heat to 400° F.

2. In a medium saucepan combine the water, salt, and the 1 tablespoon sugar. Bring to a boil; remove from heat and add flour all at once. Beat quickly with a wooden spoon to blend. Place the pan back onto medium heat and continue to beat until the mixture forms a "mass" and a film forms on the bottom of the pan (approximately 1 minute). Remove from heat and form a well in the center of the dough. Break the egg into the well and continue beat-ing until the egg has been thoroughly absorbed and the mixture is smooth.

3. With a slotted spoon remove the lime pieces from the oil and discard. Place the churro mixture into the a pastry bag fitted with a No. 6 star tip and force the dough through the tube in approximately 4-inch lengths into the hot oil. Fry until golden. Drain on paper towels. Roll in sugar and serve.

Serves 4.

BUÑUELOS
Fritters

This light, crispy sweet is wonderful served with Café de Olla (Mexican coffee; see opposite page) or hot chocolate. Try the variation with syrup for a novel dessert. For a totally untraditional version, eliminate the sugar altogether and use the buñuelos to accompany savory foods. For a smaller yield, this recipe can be reduced by half.

> 4 cups flour
> 1 teaspoon salt
> 1 teaspoon baking powder
> 2 tablespoons sugar
> ⅓ cup butter
> 2 eggs
> 1 cup milk
> Oil 1 inch deep, for frying
> ½ cup sugar
> 2 teaspoons cinnamon or pinch of ground cloves

1. Heat oil to 400° F. In a medium-sized bowl stir together flour, salt, baking powder, and the 2 tablespoons sugar; set aside. Melt butter in small saucepan and set aside.

2. In a large bowl beat eggs, mix in milk, and gradually stir in the flour, salt, baking powder, and 2 tablespoons sugar, mixing thoroughly. Add the melted butter and, with your hands, work it into the dough.

3. Turn onto lightly floured board and knead gently until smooth and elastic; roll into 30 to 50 balls. Using a rolling pin, roll each ball into a thin circle.

4. In a deep skillet heat oil until hot (400° F). Add buñuelos, a few at a time, and fry, turning to brown both sides. Drain on paper towels. Prepare sugar mixture by combining the ½ cup sugar and cinnamon. Sprinkle over buñuelos and serve.

Makes 30 to 50 buñuelos.

Variation Buñuelos are also typically served with a syrup. Prepare the buñuelos, omitting the sugar-cinnamon coating.

Syrup

  1 cup brown sugar or 6 piloncillo (Mexican raw sugar cones)
  1 cinnamon stick
  2 cups water
  Dash of dry sherry (optional)

1. Place sugar, cinnamon, and the water in a small saucepan; bring to a boil, reduce heat, and simmer 15 minutes. Stir in sherry (if used) and set aside.

2. Break the prepared buñuelos into large pieces and place in individual serving dishes. Spoon some syrup over the buñuelos and serve.

SOPAIPILLAS
Fritters

Sopaipillas are golden-fried puffs of dough. In New Mexico where they are popular, they are usually eaten with honey, as suggested here. Sopaipillas are also good served with soups, and at brunches, parties, and buffets.

  3 cups flour
  2 teaspoons baking powder
  ½ teaspoon salt
  2 tablespoons shortening
  1 cup warm water
  Oil 1½ inches deep, for frying
  Honey

1. Stir together flour, baking powder, and salt; cut in shortening with a pastry blender until coarse crumbs form. Gradually work in the water to form a pastrylike dough. Turn onto a lightly floured board. Cover with a damp cloth and allow to rest 1 hour.

2. Heat oil to 425° F in large, heavy frying pan. Divide dough in half for easier handling. Roll each ball of dough as thin as possible. Cut into 3-inch squares and fry in hot oil, pushing squares down into the oil several times so that they will puff evenly. Turn once to brown and cook until golden on both sides. Drain on paper towels.

3. Serve warm with honey.

Makes approximately 30 sopaipillas.

BEVERAGES

Cool, refreshing drinks are important to Mexicans, especially when the weather is hot and sunny. This colorful array of fruit drinks, coffees, and other beverages has unusual flair and tastes wonderful.

CAFÉ DE OLLA
Mexican pot coffee

  2 cups water
  ¼ cup Mexican coffee beans, coarsely ground
  1 large stick cinnamon
  1 tablespoon brown sugar or 1 small piloncillo (Mexican raw sugar cone), optional

1. Place water, coffee, cinnamon, and brown sugar (if used) in a saucepan and bring to a boil. Reduce heat and simmer 3 to 5 minutes. Bring to a second boil, reduce heat, and simmer another 3 to 5 minutes.

2. Strain and serve.

Serves 2.

CAFÉ CON LECHE
Coffee with milk

  2 cups strongly brewed coffee (use 2 heaping tablespoons ground coffee per cup of water)
  2 cups milk, heated
  Sugar to taste
  3 small sticks cinnamon

1. Combine coffee and hot milk. Sweeten to taste.

2. Divide evenly among 3 mugs. Place a cinnamon stick in each.

Serves 3.

CAFÉ SAN CARLOS
Mexican after-dinner coffee

Per serving:

> Whipping cream
> Sugar
> Vanilla extract
> 2 tablespoons tequila gold
> 3 tablespoons coffee liqueur
> ½ to ⅔ cup strong, hot coffee

1. Preheat the serving glass or cup by filling with hot water.

2. Whip cream until it is a spoonable consistency, but not stiff. Whip in sugar and vanilla to taste. Dry the serving glass.

3. Place tequila, coffee liqueur, and coffee into the glass.

4. Top with whipped cream and serve.

CHOCOLATE MEXICANO
Mexican hot chocolate

> 4 cups milk
> 4 ounces Mexican chocolate, crushed

1. Place milk and chocolate in a saucepan and heat over low heat, stirring.

2. Whisk until frothy or place in a warmed blender container and blend until frothy. Serve immediately.

Serves 4.

LICUADO DE MELÓN
Melon drink

> Watermelon, cantaloupe, or honeydew melon
> Juice of half a lime

Peel and seed melon; cut the melon into chunks. Place approximately 2 cups of melon at a time into a blender or food processor. Blend until liquid. Add lime juice when blending.

Add enough water to achieve the desired consistency; blend. (Start with ⅓ cup water per 2 cups melon.) Repeat with remaining melon. Serve chilled.

Number of servings will depend on your choice of melon. A medium-sized cantaloupe makes about four 1-cup servings.

LICUADO DE PIÑA
Pineapple drink

> 1 ripe pineapple, peeled and cut into chunks
> 4 cups water
> ½ cup sugar, or to taste

Place half the pineapple chunks, 2 cups of the water, and ¼ cup of the sugar in a blender and blend until smooth. Pour liquid into a pitcher. Repeat with the remaining ingredients. Chill before serving. Strain, if desired.

Makes about six 1-cup servings.

LICUADO DE FRESCA
Strawberry drink

> 4 cups fresh or frozen strawberries
> 1 to 2 cups water
> Sugar to taste

1. Place the berries, 2 cups at a time, in a blender or food processor. Add enough water to blend to a liquid.

2. Check for sweetness and add small amounts of sugar to taste. Add water to achieve the desired consistency. Blend evenly. Pour into a pitcher.

3. Repeat steps 1 and 2 with the remaining berries.

4. Serve chilled.

Makes about six 1-cup servings.

LICUADO DE PAPAYA Y NARANJA
Papaya and orange drink

> 1 ripe papaya
> 1 cup orange juice
> Juice of half a lime
> Sugar to taste

Peel and seed papaya and cut into chunks. Place in a blender with orange and lime juice. Blend until smooth; taste and add sugar, if necessary. Chill before serving.

Makes two 1-cup servings.

SANGRÍA
Wine cooler

> 1 bottle (750 ml) dry red wine
> 1 cup orange juice
> ¼ cup sugar (optional)
> 1 lime, sliced
> 1 orange, sliced
> 1 peach, or *half a pineapple*, or *half a cantaloupe*, peeled and cut into bite-sized pieces
> 1 bottle (7 oz) club soda, or to taste
> ¼ cup brandy (optional)

1. In a large glass pitcher or punch bowl, combine wine, orange juice, sugar (if used), and fruit. Chill.

2. Just before serving stir in the club soda and brandy (if used). Serve in tall glasses with lots of ice.

Serves 6.

TEQUILA

Coarse salt
Tequila
Lime wedges

The traditional sequence for drinking straight tequila: Place some salt on the back of your hand. Lick the salt, drink the tequila, and quickly bite the lime wedge.

MARGARITA

Per serving:

1 ounce white tequila
½ ounce Cointreau or Triple Sec
Juice of half a lime
½ cup crushed ice
Lime wedges
Coarse salt

1. Add tequila, Cointreau, and lime juice to crushed ice in a cocktail shaker or blender. Blend until frothy.

2. To serve, rub the rim of a chilled glass with a lime wedge. Turn the glass rim in a dish of loose salt to encrust it. Strain the margarita into the glass and serve.

SANGRITA

Juice of 1 orange
Juice of 3 limes
2 fresh jalapeños, seeded and finely chopped
2 tablespoons minced white onion
3 cups tomato juice
⅛ teaspoon salt
Tequila
Lime wedges

1. Place orange juice, lime juice, jalapeños, onion, tomato juice, and salt in a blender container; cover and blend briefly on low speed. Chill.

2. Serve accompanied by a small glass of tequila and a lime wedge. Sip the sangrita and tequila alternately; then bite the lime.

Serves 4.

There is an incredible variety of liquid refreshments served in Mexico. Tequila with lime, margaritas, fresh fruit licuados, and sangría make a colorful array of beverages.

INDEX

Note: Page numbers in italics refer to illustrations separated from recipe text.

U.S. MEASURE AND METRIC MEASURE CONVERSION CHART

		Formulas for Exact Measures			Rounded Measures for Quick Reference		
	Symbol	**When you know:**	**Multiply by**	**To find:**			
Mass (Weight)	oz	ounces	28.35	grams	1 oz		= 30 g
	lb	pounds	0.45	kilograms	4 oz		= 115 g
	g	grams	0.035	ounces	8 oz		= 225 g
	kg	kilograms	2.2	pounds	16 oz	= 1 lb	= 450 g
					32 oz	= 2 lb	= 900 g
					36 oz	= 2¼ lb	= 1,000 g (1 kg)
Volume	tsp	teaspoons	5.0	milliliters	¼ tsp	= 1/24 oz	= 1 ml
	tbsp	tablespoons	15.0	milliliters	½ tsp	= 1/12 oz	= 2 ml
	fl oz	fluid ounces	29.57	milliliters	1 tsp	= 1/6 oz	= 5 ml
	c	cups	0.24	liters	1 tbsp	= ½ oz	= 15 ml
	pt	pints	0.47	liters	1 c	= 8 oz	= 250 ml
	qt	quarts	0.95	liters	2 c (1 pt)	= 16 oz	= 500 ml
	gal	gallons	3.785	liters	4 c (1 qt)	= 32 oz	= 1 l.
	ml	milliliters	0.034	fluid ounces	4 qt (1 gal)	= 128 oz	= 3¾ l.
Length	in.	inches	2.54	centimeters	3/8 in.	= 1 cm	
	ft	feet	30.48	centimeters	1 in.	= 2.5 cm	
	yd	yards	0.9144	meters	2 in.	= 5 cm	
	mi	miles	1.609	kilometers	2½ in.	= 6.5 cm	
	km	kilometers	0.621	miles	12 in. (1 ft)	= 30 cm	
	m	meters	1.094	yards	1 yd	= 90 cm	
	cm	centimeters	0.39	inches	100 ft	= 30 m	
					1 mi	= 1.6 km	
Temperature	° F	Fahrenheit	5/9 (after subtracting 32)	Celsius	32° F	= 0° C	
					68 °F	= 20° C	
	° C	Celsius	9/5 (then add 32)	Fahrenheit	212° F	= 100° C	
Area	$in.^2$	square inches	6.452	square centimeters	1 $in.^2$	= 6.5 cm^2	
	ft^2	square feet	929.0	square centimeters	1 ft^2	= 930 cm^2	
	yd^2	square yards	8,361.0	square centimeters	1 yd^2	= 8,360 cm^2	
	a	acres	0.4047	hectares	1 a	= 4,050 m^2	